"The narratives in this book are raw, honest, inspirational and devastating. To hold a life's fate in your hands can be nothing else. These are the true stories of people who have been caught up in the life and death battle known as 'choice' in our modern world. These are the voices we desperately need to hear from as the abortion industry cranks forward with little regard for human life, born or pre-born. I sincerely thank the authors of these stories who dared to expose themselves to the world in the hope of reaching out to someone else who may be considering abortion, or who is dealing with the destruction that abortion leaves in its wake. Your bravery will save lives. Raw, honest, inspirational and devastating. That's what you'll find in these pages. A beautiful read."

—Laura Klassen
Human Rights Activist,
Founder and Director of CHOICE42

"This book should be in every crisis pregnancy center, readily available for anyone who is contemplating abortion or has had one. *Unborn. Untold.* is a testament to God's deliverance and healing power, and the beauty of the life He gives."

—Brad Burke, MD
Author, *An MD Examines* series

"If there hadn't been a law against abortion when I was born, I wouldn't be here today. I was conceived in stress; I don't really know who my father was, but I caused a lot of problems for my birth mother in arriving as an unplanned pregnancy into her body, invading her future. So much so that she felt she had no choice but to end the pregnancy and attempted an abortion four times. Somehow through the goodness of God my life was spared. So my heart is not only for the unborn children but for the women who feel they have no support, no resources, no options. I long for them to receive the message that, whatever happened in the past or whatever they face in the present, God's grace is sufficient. There is hope and there is healing, and I pray they find both in the pages of this book."

—Lorna Dueck
Crossroads CEO & Host of Context, Beyond the Headlines

"Ruth Coghill has provided a voice for many walking the post-abortion journey, enabling them to share their stories of how, in the aftermath of loss and anguish, they were able to find hope and healing. *Unborn. Untold.* is a heart-wrenching must-read for all those whose lives have been impacted by abortion."

—Lois Benham-Smith
Executive Director of Atwell Centre:
Pregnancy Options Support -
Providing Hope, Compassion, and Information

"This book is long overdue, as it will reveal the reality of the fear, pain, trauma, and deep-rooted guilt and loss of abortion. The brave women and men who have shared their heartfelt stories with honesty and vulnerability are to be commended for speaking out and revealing the horrific truth of their experiences. The circumstances that led them to abort and the consequences of taking a life cannot be ignored, and are brought to light in a heart-wrenching, incredible way, story after story. This book touched my heart and I am overwhelmed with grief more than ever by the genocide of the unborn and the women who felt there was no other way for them. This read will motivate you to do more to fight for life and believe that you can make a difference. If you have had an abortion and are struggling with guilt and need to find forgiveness and grace, you will find it in these pages."

—Cathy Ciaramitaro
President of Windsor Life Centre
Pastor and Teacher
Co-leader of Open Bible Faith Fellowship

"More than ever, these stories must be shared! I am so grateful for the courage and honesty of these beautiful and brave women and men in opening up their souls and sharing with us their heartache, their healing, and, most importantly, their hope. Thanks also to Ruth Coghill for compiling these inspiring stories and sharing them with an often disillusioned world. Please do yourself a favour—pull up a chair, grab a box of Kleenex, and get ready to be inspired and blessed. Even more importantly, do someone else a favour and pick up an extra copy or two and pass this priceless book along to anyone you know who has either experienced, or has ever considered, an abortion. These stories will help all who read them recognize the beauty of choosing life, and illuminate to all the unquestionable power of forgiveness."

—Rev. Jeff Bell
Trentside Baptist Church
Bobcaygeon, Ontario, Canada

"Truth meets grace in this beautiful unfolding of hearts poured out, recounting God's healing and redemption in the lives of those impacted by abortion. Thankful to have this book as a reference to minister hope to each client I work with whose life has been touched by this all too familiar pain. I look forward to each one discovering God's healing grace through the pages of *Unborn. Untold.*"

—Tanya Glanzman, LPC
My Father's Daughter Ministries

"In all the noise and opinions on the abortion issue today, Ruth Coghill has done the important work in this book of letting us hear directly from those who have been through an abortion, have been pressured to have one, or have been affected by the choice of someone close to them who has made that choice. Their voices and stories need to be heard. A necessary read for our times."

—Pastor Tim Gibb
Senior Pastor, Bethel Pentecostal Church
Sarnia, Ontario, Canada

Unborn.
Untold.

True Stories of Abortion
and God's Healing Grace

RUTH COGHILL
WITH SARA DAVISON

UNBORN. UNTOLD.

Copyright © 2019 by Ruth Coghill with Sara Davison

Printed in Canada

Print ISBN: 978-1-4866-1893-4
eBook ISBN: 978-1-4866-1894-1

Word Alive Press
119 De Baets Street, Winnipeg, MB R2J 3R9
www.wordalivepress.ca

Cataloguing in Publication may be obtained through Library and Archives Canada

Dedication

To all those who have dedicated their lives to supporting women experiencing a crisis pregnancy or post-abortion, offering them grace and compassion and showing them there is love, acceptance, healing, and hope in Jesus Christ.

And to the precious ones who have no stones to mark their lives, but who are held tightly in the arms of Jesus.

Contents

For you created my inmost being;
you knit me together in my mother's womb.
I praise you because I am fearfully and wonderfully made;
your works are wonderful,
I know that full well.
My frame was not hidden from you
when I was made in the secret place,
when I was woven together in the depths of the earth.
Your eyes saw my unformed body;
all the days ordained for me were written in your book
before one of them came to be.

—Psalm 139:13-16

Foreword

Every person is unique and important. So, every person's story is unique and important. This book contains stories of experiences with difficult pregnancies, abortion, and Christian faith. Stories shared in the hopes that they will help others.

These stories were hard for me to read. Some of the women and men in this book experienced evil at the hands of others and were deeply wounded. Many were pressured to make decisions they did not want to make by partners, family members, or medical professionals who should have been caring and compassionate but were not. These stories reminded me, as my work often does, that the world is broken, and people can do such damage to themselves and those they care about.

But in these stories about hurt and regret there is also courage, healing, and forgiveness. I know those telling these stories hope their experiences help you find courage and healing for the challenges you face along your journey in our broken world.

If you are facing an unexpected pregnancy, take the time you need and seek the supports necessary for your choice to be your choice and no one else's. Your life will change, no matter what choice you make. Don't let anyone push you into decisions or make decisions for you. You are strong, unique, and important.

If you are unsure what choice is best for you, seek out people you trust to talk through your options with you. That may be a family member, friend, or teacher who values you and with whom you feel safe. It may be a doctor, nurse, or midwife. It could be a leader in a faith community. In many cities there are Pregnancy Centres with volunteers trained to explore options with you. You might need to talk to several people before you are ready to decide. No matter who it is you share your struggle with, your conversations with them need to allow you to explore who you are, how this pregnancy will change your life, and how your values and experiences can help you make the decisions that are best for you. If anyone pressures you, or tries to tell you what to do, then walk away and find another person to talk to.

If you have made decisions about pregnancy that you now regret, I recommend that you also find the right person to talk to and work through your experience. Don't let anyone tell you how you ought to feel or think about your experience. You and your experiences are unique. If you have been wounded, you are strong and important enough to seek healing. The stories in this book involve Christian faith as part of journeys of healing, and that can be your experience as well. Receiving and giving forgiveness is central to the Jesus story and is a powerful source of healing.

You are unique, important, and strong. Find the people and supports you need to make the best decisions you can for your future or to find healing from past decisions you regret.

Dr. Dan Reilly is a physician, educator, and leader. Through the practice of obstetrics and gynecology, and formal and informal teaching, speaking, and advising, Dr. Reilly serves hundreds of patients, students, colleagues, and members of the public each year. He has taught on a wide variety of topics related to medicine, administration, ethics, and teaching. To learn more see www.danreilly.ca or contact him at dreilly@mcmaster.ca

A Letter from the National House of Prayer

Imagine yourself standing on the lower lawn of Parliament Hill in Ottawa on a sunny, early morning, amidst a sea of tiny pink and blue flags planted in the ground.

A volunteer is still placing the final flags when a leading Member of Parliament on the way to his office stops and asks, "What do these flags represent?"

"The flags recognize all the babies aborted in Canada in any given year," he is told.

For a moment he stares at the flags. Then, in a hushed voice, he comments, "It's a striking visual display," before he turns and walks away.

It is a striking display. A striking, shocking display. The sheer numbers—a hundred thousand tiny markers—sweep away breath. Break the heart.

Now imagine all those tiny flags replaced by hundreds of thousands of joyful Canadians who gather on the lawn of Parliament in Ottawa wearing pink or blue T-shirts, thankful for the life-affirming laws in Canada. Celebrating life instead of marking death.

Perhaps one day.

The National House of Prayer has sought to advance prayer for, and to promote, ministries and organizations on the front lines in raising awareness of the devastating reality of abortion in our nation.

Unborn. Untold. gathers stories of those still living with the pain of abortion in the hope of showing those who understand that pain all too well that there is grace and healing in Jesus Christ. The real-life stories represented in this book can be used of God to touch those who need to hear such a message.

We join with all who shared their experiences within these pages to offer the important message that, whether or not governments pass a law making abortion illegal, the church—you and I through Christ working in us—can offer the love, grace, support, and options that will show women in desperate situations that there is a better choice, for them and for the precious life they carry.

We stand with you,
Rob and Fran Parker
The National House of Prayer

Preface

Dearest Reader,

I believe this book has found its way into your hands for a specific purpose. Perhaps you will find yourself somewhere in these pages, as if someone knew your history and was telling your story. You may possibly know someone who needs to read these powerful stories and you can pass it on to them.

It was so brave of these precious women and men to risk sharing their personal experiences. Every facet of their memories is held as a jewel in the Father's hands; all are a unique mosaic of intricate detail, personalities, histories, healing, and ways of processing life.

If you have had an abortion, or have been part of the story of someone who has, let me assure you that there is hope, and the Father holds *your* story as well. A myriad of different thoughts, emotions, and memories, all filtered through the lens of perception and belief systems, may impact you as the words lift off the page and into your heart.

When traumatic events happen, by our own choice or through the choices of others, the ripple effect can become a wave and perhaps even a tsunami that rips through our lives, affecting our future and the future of those around us. At other times, this ripple can feel like a swift undercurrent threatening to pull us under at any moment, leaving us to flail about to keep above the waves. It's exhausting.

One would think time would take care of the feelings and memories, but they just don't seem to go away. They set an atmosphere in and around us, creating what feels like a cesspool of emotions that leads to a stagnant pond where very little grows.

There is a saying that "time heals all things." Yet for many, years after a traumatic event they still feel the same rawness as if it happened yesterday. The truth is, time alone does *not* heal all things, especially those things that have been buried in the dark.

Uncovering years of secrets, choices, feelings, and tendrils of events that have attached themselves and come close to strangling the life out of us and our relationships is difficult, but crucial for freedom. It is a journey that cannot be fully captured in the chapter of a book, but I applaud each contributor for having the courage to make the attempt.

I believe by reading these true-life events, a hope that healing is possible will be stirred. You may be challenged to take a few steps toward the beginning of a journey of healing in your own life, or to go deeper into a place of peace, hope, and joy you never even knew existed.

God wants to come into the middle of every chapter of our lives. Nothing is too difficult, appalling, or unforgiveable to Him. God wants to hear all of it, heal all of it, and absorb all of the pain into Himself. Only the light of Christ shining on our wounds can bring the depth of healing that is needed for life transformation.

He created us, spirit, soul, and body, and desires for us to be healthy and whole in order for the fruit of the Spirit to manifest itself in our everyday lives and touch the lives of others.

No longer a slave to the past, with lies and old behaviours, we can then move forward into the future, believing what the Word says about us and who He is in our life.

Freedom is a choice. No one is excluded from the promise of Jesus that *"... the truth will set you free"* (John 8:32).

May each one of you experience this healing and freedom as you read the stories in this book.

Joy to you,
Joy Presland, Life Coach

Please Tell My Story
by Ruth Coghill

"Please tell my story." Rebecca* looked at me longingly, tears running down her face. "I'm too old to tell it now—I have children and grandchildren."

I'd grown to love this dear friend who'd attended my Bible study for a number of years. Rebecca was gracious, kind, and full of fun, and I always looked forward to being with her, enjoying her positive outlook on life and her love of learning God's precepts. I never noticed the pain behind the smile, the laugh.

One morning she quietly requested a coffee time with me. The date had been set, and now we sat on the love seat in my living room. "This is the most painful thing I've ever done... to go back in my mind and recount the events and circumstances around the terrible sin I committed."

My heartbeat quickened as the muscles in her face tightened, and emotions so deeply ingrained spilled out in waves of sadness and grief. Unbearable pain etched deep lines and wrinkles on her beautiful countenance. I listened, keenly aware that even the retelling was gut-wrenching. She told me of her engagement to a young man and the discovery that she was pregnant. Much against her fiancé's wishes, Rebecca decided to abort their baby.

I'd never given much thought to abortion except in a judgmental way.

Now, as a speaker, I was meeting women who were sharing with me their mental anguish over having chosen to end their pregnancies. Some whispered in my ear in the church foyer on a Sunday morning, and yet another chose a private meeting place. I listened with care. My heart softening, I opened my closed mind and set out to help those who need forgiveness and understanding. God would have answers for the many women who had hidden their secret of abortion as my friend had.

Today women are encouraged to demand their rights, to exercise their choices over their bodies. But where do the mother's rights end and the baby's begin?

"What right did I have to end a life God had created?" Rebecca's eyes searched mine, although I understood no answer was expected. We both knew that whether a child is conceived in love or lust, according to Psalm 139:13-14, only God can weave a precious little one in its mother's womb. *"For you created my inmost being; you knit me together in my mother's womb. I praise you because I am fearfully and wonderfully made; your works are wonderful, I know that full well."* Only God can take the ashes of a rape and create a beautiful life, one that holds promise, potential, and purpose. He is the God of restoration. But does anyone else have any rights over the unborn child? What about the father? Of course there are some men who do not want the responsibility, just the ten minutes of pleasure, but that's not always the case.

Rebecca's realization of how much she had hurt her fiancé hit her years later. "He was devastated that I didn't want his baby. We parted company and I never saw him again. I not only sinned against God but against this man."

> Today women are encouraged to demand their rights, to exercise their choices over their bodies. But where do the mother's rights end and the baby's begin?

I began to consider every father who hadn't been given any choice in the matter of his baby's death. Were some of those broken hearts also sitting in the pews at my church? And what about the siblings, the grandparents, and everyone who longed for a child but would never know the miracle of the womb? It has been said that we don't come *from our parents* but *through our parents from God.*

Rebecca eventually married, and God blessed her with children and grandchildren. Still, deep inside, she agonized over the fact that she didn't deserve children since she had given one up so easily. For over forty years she carried this heavy burden in her heart. Fear of rejection, consequences, and shame held her in such bondage that she believed she could never be free. Oh, the debilitating pain of guilt, often considered the number one destroyer of self-worth. It eats away at the core of our being, screaming, *Loser, you will never amount to anything.*

"One Sunday at church, the minister preached on grace." Rebecca leaned against the cushions on the love seat. *"For it is by grace you have been saved, by faith—and this is not from yourselves, is the gift from God…"* (Ephesians 2:8b). She toyed with the fringes of the blanket tossed over the arm of the seat. "He has forgiven me. But how do I forgive myself? It's difficult, although it's easier since I openly confessed my sin to God, because of His incredible grace."

Rebecca shared a message for those to whom she wanted me to tell her story. "Dear reader, if you are living with the same guilt and burden I was, pray for God's forgiveness. He knows your weaknesses. There are no secrets from Him, but He is a forgiving Father. If through my testimony I save one life, touch one heart, or spare just one person from the pain I've endured, it will be worth what I've been through."

I now loved this dear friend with a new kind of love. Her confession to me in no way lessened my love for her but helped me realize again that we are all imperfect people wanting to live for God but burdened and held captive by our sins.

Rebecca has walked that deep valley of life after an abortion. She wants others to listen to her experience and learn from it. "If you know of someone who is thinking of taking a wee innocent life, I beg you, don't let them do it. The hurt they will have to live with is very hard to bear. Pray for guidance, asking God for help."

We said our goodbyes at the door, hugging each other with renewed appreciation of the importance of a safe place to pour out the deep hurts of our hearts and a deeper awareness of God's unfathomable mercy and love.

For years I've kept her secret, waiting for the right time to share it but knowing I had to do something to help my friend. The gift of her story, of her trust, carried with it a charge to pass it along, to use it to help others. Now is the time. I have done what I could and what she asked... I've told her story.

But Rebecca's story is only one of countless others. I'm so thankful that you have picked up this book because, no matter your story, when you read the ones these precious women and men recount, you will know that you are not alone. You may have had an abortion and, like Rebecca, carried the shame and guilt for many years. I pray that, as she did, you will find God's grace and forgiveness and your burden will be lifted. You will meet other women and men who struggle with deep pain and regret. At the end of this book, you will find principles, written by psychologist Libby Skidmore, to guide you through a journey to healing.

Perhaps you were not given the choice to keep your baby. Pregnant at fifteen years old, Candace* was frightened and alone. Her doctor recommended an abortion. "I was shocked at his suggestion but didn't know what to do," she acknowledged to me. As she was five weeks short of her sixteenth birthday, she needed the consent of at least one parent.

Months earlier, Candace's father had imparted a strong message to his girls, "Any daughter of mine who comes home pregnant will be out on her ear faster than a blink."

"I yearned to keep my baby, but I couldn't see it as a possibility. I cried all night then just pushed the idea out of my thoughts." Agonizing over her options, she finally told her mother. "Crushed and in shock, my mom simply wept, a wedge driven between us." Candace's mom insisted she tell her father. "Dad immediately called and made the appointment for my abortion."

Since she accepted the responsibility for her situation, Candace didn't feel she had any right to say anything. "It hurt that there was no discussion about how I felt or what I thought. Dad and I had always been close, but his reaction was cold and the discussion over." A special father-daughter bond was severed that day. Added to Candace's personal pain was the emotional and mental trauma she'd caused her parents and the broken trust of relationship.

Her appointment approached too quickly. An overnight stay in the hospital gave Candace time to consider what she faced the following morning. From the time she'd been old enough, she never passed up an opportunity to babysit and took every child-related course in high school. "I always dreamed of being a mom."

Early in the morning the nurse awakened her, gave her medication, and soon she was wheeled on the gurney to wait her turn. Panic welled up inside when the enormity of what she was about to do hit. Changing her mind, she asked to speak to her doctor, crying, "I can't kill my baby!" Being strapped down, her only option was to shake her head, repeating her desperate plea.

The doctor responded, "You'll be okay," and gave her arm a gentle pat. Except that she wasn't okay. She passed out, only to wake up and discover that she had ended the life of her first child.

Candace confessed, "It's over, only it's never over. I push it aside, but it never leaves. How much I'd give to reverse what I did. I'd never asked anything like this before, but I asked God to forgive me. It took me a long time to accept that He did."

When she finally married and gave birth to her first son, Candace rejoiced over God's mercy in allowing her to conceive again. Sharing her story has enabled her to discover God's healing and peace. She emphasizes, "I want to help others going through the same pain and confusion. My hope is to be able to offer women who are contemplating abortion all the information and options before making any choice."

Well over four million Canadian stories, some told, so many others kept secret, have been woven since the first abortion clinic opened in 1969 in Montreal. The Supreme Court struck down the abortion law in 1988, and since that time there have been no abortion laws in our beautiful nation.

Dr. Henry Morgentaler personally performed over 100,000 abortions. He was named a Member of the Order of Canada in October, 2008, and said he was "proud" and "honoured" to be able to live out his dream of creating a "better and more humane society" (*Maranatha News* October 2008). The question is: Who gets this "better" and "more humane" life—the mother who terminates the pregnancy, the father, the grandmother who holds her daughter's hand as she aborts her first grandchild, or the baby itself?

My friends Candace and Rebecca wouldn't use either *better* or *humane* to describe their experiences.

On January 8, 2019, I snuggled our new grandson, Odin Alexander, barely four hours old, and praised God once again for the miracle of life. Odin is grandchild number thirteen, eleven with us and two little ones already in heaven with Jesus, but the beauty and miracle of birth never gets tiring for this Nana.

Our youngest son, Alexander James, is now a proud father. He wanted to hold Odin again and gently removed him from the cradle of my arms. The longing in his daddy's eyes spoke of his love for his baby and reminded me how long he and Jody had waited for their first child.

I stood still, momentarily transported three decades back in time when I was pregnant with A.J.—a moment etched in my mind forever. I sat in a hospital room in London, Ontario, where I was undergoing tests to determine potential threats to our fourth unborn child. In this professional and very immaculate environment, I heard the doctor-counsellor offer me an abortion. Frightening thoughts and fears fought for a spot in my scrambled mind, and then I mentally covered my ears and blocked out all sounds for the duration of my appointment.

Bob and I had always wanted four children, but we had planned to have them all in one decade. Our two sons, Scott and Kevin, sixteen and fourteen, along with our eight-year-old daughter Heather, were the delight of our lives. I had loved being a stay-at-home mom for those early years and had only recently donned my red suit and hat for an interview to return to my teaching career. Shocked, I discovered that my fatigue and general lack of energy were not menopause but a fourth pregnancy.

I told Bob my secret and he immediately responded, "Unplanned does not mean unwanted."

In the months that followed that hospital visit, I had to do some serious soul searching. Could it be that easy to get rid of your baby? In a professional setting? If I hadn't had a husband by my side to support, clothe, and feed this little one, would I have given in to a quick fix? I desperately wanted to say that I'd never succumb to the brutal act of abortion, but I agonized over the different circumstances each woman faces and the choices that follow.

Watching my son now as he cradled our tiny grandchild, a lump rose in my throat and a tear tickled my lower eyelid. Before me I witnessed two generations of blessing, father and son, the powerful effect of one decision to choose life.

I have met many women who made the decision to keep their babies, in spite of very difficult circumstances. And their stories need to be told. Stories that demonstrate the powerful ripple effect of our choices. That tell of moms, dads, siblings, grandparents who long for those babies.

Dan Allender writes in his book *To Be Told*, "God is our Authority and also the Author of our lives. As He continues to write our stories, He will continue to use our past experiences to open up our future[1]." The author reminds us that, "Your life and mine not only reveal who we are, but they also reveal who God is."

God will never waste our pain but will use it for His purposes. He loves, forgives, heals, and restores. God makes it possible for all of us to have a fresh start, taking the ashes of our past and recreating them for His purposes. Our stories bring glory to God and healing to others when we share them.

As Allender puts it, "Your story helps reveal the Greatest Story, the story that God is telling about himself. God intends for each of us to live for a great glory, and a greater story, than our own."

And that's a story that needs to be told.

---

1   Allender, Dan B. *To Be Told: Know Your Story, Shape Your Life*. Waterbrook Press, 2005.

one

No More Hiding

by Amy Jackson

It started slowly for me. One bad choice, then another, and another. I grew up in a loving, healthy, happy home. With two older sisters, I always had someone to talk to, ride bikes with, or challenge to an epic game of Stock Ticker. Our whole family enjoyed camping. Every summer we set out for our annual three-week camping trip. Everyone squashed into the car with the old camper—canvas held together by yards of duct tape—in tow.

We enjoyed campfires and marshmallows every night, as well as board games in the dining tent and my favourite... fishing with my dad! Dad and I would spend hours out on the lake bass fishing. Sometimes we'd get up before dawn, slip the canoe into the calm water, and enjoy the peace and beauty of a sunrise over the lake.

I'm fortunate to have such childhood memories. I felt safe. I felt loved. Yet at the age of seventeen I was an alcoholic and a drug addict. There was no abuse I needed to escape. No anger I needed to run from. No pain I was trying to bury. What I did have was a deep sense of not being enough. I felt I needed to be stronger, smarter, prettier—"just me" wasn't enough. I didn't measure up to what I thought I should be. The trouble was that I fully based my self-worth on what others thought of me. I became obsessed with how my friends viewed me. Did they think I was strong? Smart? Pretty? Tough? Funny? I was all too eager to become what I believed everyone else wanted me to be.

My weekend drinking increased until my parents voiced their concern. They cautioned me. They warned me. During late-night conversations around the kitchen table, they pleaded with me to accept help. Rather than listening with open, fearless honesty, I ran. I ran from the uncomfortable feeling of being wrong, of being out of control, of being addicted and unable to stop. I moved out and rented a little one-bedroom apartment downtown. After that my destructive behaviour escalated. I didn't have to try and hide my drug use or drinking. Every day, every hour, whenever I wanted, I could get high. And that's exactly what I did.

I never went a day without a hit of something, or a few hours without a drink. I endured abusive relationships just to get high. I woke up in stairwells, in places I didn't know, with people I didn't know. I was raped and assaulted. Often I would go days without sleeping or eating. The alcohol and drugs didn't deliver what they promised me. In the beginning, their effects were fun—I felt invincible, confident. When I was drunk and high, I finally felt as though I was enough.

But the promise of beauty, excitement, and strength soon crumbled. It didn't take long for me to realize that those feelings were fake; there was nothing worthwhile or lasting about them. Addiction stripped me of everything—my morals, my values, self-worth, and identity. Instead of glamour I had ugliness. Instead of peace I had sleepless nights. Instead of strength I was overwhelmed by weakness, helpless to fight against the addiction. It consumed my thoughts, like a monster that overcame me. Embraces that I thought expressed love and meaning turned into empty sex. I wanted to go back... back to the truth, back to being honest and real. But I couldn't stop myself. As far as I was concerned, I was in too far to change.

Then it happened. The unbearable. The unthinkable. I became pregnant. I thought maybe if I just ignored it, pretended as though it wasn't happening, things would go back to normal. I tried to make sense of how I was feeling physically, devise other possible reasons for it. Was I hitting it too hard lately, partying every night? That was a given. Three grams of cocaine weren't going as far for me as they used to. Or maybe I was simply getting run down and sick like I had before, many times. I wasn't convinced. Every morning I threw up, and I couldn't remember when my last period was.

Finally, I could no longer deny the truth. Tears streamed down my face. *This can't be happening to me. It isn't possible; don't even think about it because it's not true.* The thoughts echoed like screams through my head.

Days went by, then weeks. I was tired all the time. Morning sickness hit me like clockwork, and I cried during every solitary moment. I couldn't put it off any longer. I needed to know for sure.

After buying a cheap pregnancy test from the drugstore, I headed home. I waited the allotted three minutes, like the box said, and then I waited four, five, six minutes. *I can't, I can't look at it.* I knew what the result would be, but I didn't want to see the proof staring back at me. Finally, fearing that the results might not be accurate if I waited any longer, I walked into the bathroom with closed eyes. When I opened them and saw the double lines, my worst fears came true.

The strength in my legs left me, and I crashed to the floor. "No, no, no, no, no," I kept repeating through my sobs. "Please God, no." I cried so hard I couldn't catch my breath. The room was spinning—I had to get out of the bathroom. I crawled along the floor and up the steps to the living room, tears still coursing down my cheeks. I was crying from a place deep down inside. The place that I had kept locked up for so long was now split wide open.

My soul was raw with emotion. Loneliness, sorrow, pain, and despair all came rushing out. It was too much for me to handle. Unable to stop the tears, I lay on the floor, curled up in a little ball holding my knees. I was crying for more than my situation. I was crying for my lost soul, my lost life. I was crying for the person that I had let myself become.

Hours later I awoke, still on the floor. My face was wet, my throat raw, and nose bleeding. Clambering to my feet, I stumbled back to the bathroom to clean myself up. Disgust filled me as I stared at the face in the mirror. Tears welled again. *Keep it together*, a voice inside my head said. *You can fix this and no one will ever know. It'll be like it never happened.*

I shook the thought away and mixed a strong drink. Then I grabbed my stash and popped a hit of ecstasy. The thoughts in my head subsided, but still, I didn't want to be alone with them. Hands shaking and vision blurred, I called up a friend. Never one to admit my problems, I told her I wanted to party. As usual, within minutes my apartment had been transformed into a club. Friends came out of the woodwork, drinks were poured, joints rolled, and the music cranked.

While in my bedroom changing, I closed my soul off, buried my emotions deep, and emerged as the Amy that everyone knew. I slipped back into the mold that I had allowed everyone else to shape for me. But inside I was slowly dying. My dark, dried-up soul longed for fresh life-giving water.

For days I walked around heartbroken and confused, my mind constantly racing. I couldn't sleep. I couldn't think. I felt so lost I didn't know where to begin to deal with what was going on. I needed to talk to someone. I needed someone to put their arms around me, someone to help me, someone to love me. Little did I know that Jesus was standing outside the door of my soul, quietly knocking, longing to throw his loving arms around me. I had become so lost I barely knew His voice.

Instead of listening to His soft whisper, I bought into the lies. He doesn't love you. Not anymore. Not after this. I wanted to run to my mother and tell her, but my head was so full of lies. You can't. You can't tell anyone. What would people think of you? You have already put your family through so much; this would break them. They don't deserve to be burdened with this. It's your mess—you fix it.

I tried to stop the constant battle that raged inside my head, but I couldn't. The lies just kept coming. You would be a horrible mother. You'd never be able to stay sober. How could you afford a child? You can't keep it and marry him; you'd be stuck forever. You would be this woman you detested, this worthless hopeless shell of a person forever trapped. Forever an addict, living this life permanently.

No. That wasn't going to happen to me. The lies started to make more sense. You only have one real option: have an abortion and things can go back to normal. No one will ever find out. Day by day the lies chipped away at my spirit. Slowly my strength of mind faded, and I found myself seriously considering abortion. I knew it was murder. I knew it was appalling. Most of all, I knew no one could ever know.

I booked the appointment.

"Follow me, please." At the clinic, I did as I was told and followed the nurse down the hallway to a small curtained-off space. "You can change into your gown here," she said. Pulling the curtain shut she marched back down the hall.

I moved as if I were on auto pilot, slowly undressing and slipping on the gown. My mind was blank, my emotions numb. I wouldn't allow myself to think or feel. Standing in the small room I could hear the quiet sobs and whispered reassurances of the couple next to me. How many other babies … ? *No. I won't think of that. I can't think of that!*

I walked over to the chair and started folding my clothes. Without warning, the curtains were pulled open.

"Follow me, please," the nurse said again.

I followed obediently. We passed another woman in a gown. She glanced at me, then quickly away, her wet red eyes staring at the floor as she followed her escort. I felt nothing when I saw her. I'd retreated into survival mode, doing what I needed to do to survive this horrible experience.

We turned left and entered another room where several nurses busily checked gauges and adjusted instruments.

"Sit here."

I did as I was told. The doctor made some comment about the weather. I said nothing. A nurse gently patted my hand and told me to relax. When instructed to, I lay down and stared blankly at the ceiling. A horrible loud noise filled the room. My body burned with pain, but I didn't move. I couldn't take my eyes off the ceiling as I didn't want to take in all that was going on around me. I wanted it to be ten years earlier when I was a little girl fishing with my dad, happy, innocent, and carefree, full of honesty and joy. I couldn't face it now. Not what I was doing, not what I'd became. Tears welled in my eyes and poured down my cheeks. I couldn't hold them back. Before I knew it, I was sobbing uncontrollably.

"Hold her still," commanded the doctor.

As the nurses held me down, the crying slowly subsided and numbness closed over me once again.

The nurse led me down the hallway. Again we passed a woman in a gown. We said nothing as our eyes, sad and hopeless, met.

As I lay on the bed, nauseated, another nurse bustled in and injected something into my thigh, then gave me a couple of pills. She left without saying a word. I stared at the ceiling, clutching my abdomen and feeling as though my insides were on fire. I could hear the crying of women around me, but my tears had dried up. I would cry no more tears, speak no more words, feel no more emotion. I would lock this agony deep inside and never think of it again.

Or so I thought. Even without words or thoughts, my abortion experience refused to be buried. It was a dark agony inside me, and out of it grew a deep hatred of myself. I became the empty shell of a woman I had feared I would. Plagued with nightmares of children and babies I couldn't save. Breaking into a cold sweat and uncontrollable tears anytime I had a doctor's appointment. Depression grabbed hold of me. I became convinced I didn't deserve to live, not after what I had done. I stockpiled pills, making plans and then an attempt to end it all, only to wake up the next morning covered in vomit but still alive.

Finally, I was evicted from my apartment for not paying rent. I had nowhere to go, except back home. So that's where I went. I can see now, looking back, that God was directing my steps. For it was while living at home that I started going to church again with my parents. I sat in the pew at the back, a hopeless addict with tears streaming down her face. Wearing a shirt that was too tight and a skirt that was too short.

With shaky hands I clutched my tissue. I knew of God, I knew He had once loved me. But now a mountain of ugliness stood between me and God. An impenetrable wall of shame and guilt surrounded me, for I had knowingly done such horrible things. Such unspeakable and appalling things. My hands had innocent blood on them. Acknowledging that would rip my heart from my chest and crush my soul to dust.

So I continued on in my silence. Drowning my thoughts with drugs and alcohol. Refusing to lay my secrets open and bare before God. I lived two lives—part of me desperate for God and part of me a hopeless addict. Too afraid that if I let God into my shame He would reject me. Too afraid to trust Him with my secrets. After all, it wasn't as though I didn't know abortion was wrong; I knew and I chose it anyway. My choice had not only taken the life of my precious baby, it was now slowly killing me too.

But God is patient, gentle, and loving toward us. And one Sunday He spoke directly to my heart: "I love you. I will not forsake you. I will not cast you aside."

A picture formed in my mind as clear as day—the picture of Jesus on the cross, His body bloody and mangled. God saw to the very core of my being, dirty, ugly, and shameful. God had seen me, the choices I would make, the horrible things I would do. And He still sent His precious Son Jesus to die on the cross for me. Why would He do that if He didn't love me?

My heart was broken and filled with joy in the same moment. Broken knowing my sins had crucified Jesus, that Jesus had taken what I deserved. Yet profoundly overjoyed by such unmatched love, love for me, despite my sin.

"*Therefore, there is now no condemnation for those who are in Christ Jesus, because through Christ Jesus the law of the Spirit who gives life has set you free from the law of sin and death*" (Romans 8:1-2).

Before the pastor even said the words, I knew I would be going to the front of the church, standing in front of everyone. He gave the invitation for those who needed Jesus to save them to come forward. I went. My feet felt heavy as I moved down the aisle, my vision blurred by tears. "Forgive me, Jesus, forgive me," I whispered through my sobs.

> God had seen me, the choices I would make, the horrible things I would do. And He still sent His precious Son Jesus to die on the cross for me.

As I stood at the front, I felt a warm embrace around me. Tears poured down my face as my nose ran. With no thought for how I looked, or for who was watching, I raised my hands high, gave everything over, and knelt before the One who had never left my side.

Over the months that followed, I experienced pain, grief, understanding, and grace. God guided my steps to the Peterborough Pregnancy Support Services. There I had a chance to participate in a post-abortive recovery program where I learned about the effects of Post-Traumatic Stress Disorder. Step by step, layer by layer, I exposed my agony. Digging down deep through the shame, the lies, and the guilt. God's word became a healing balm over my shredded heart as He walked me from secrecy, to honesty, to freedom.

Three verses had a profound effect on me during this time. I was moved by the idea that God records our suffering when I read, "*You keep track of all my sorrows. You have collected all my tears in your bottle. You have recorded each one in your book*" (Psalm 56:8 NLT). And by the hope offered by the Apostle Paul's words, "*Therefore, if anyone is in Christ, the new creation has come: The old has gone, the new is here!*" (2 Corinthians 5:17 ESV) and John's assurance, "*For God did not send his son into the world to condemn the world, but to save the world through him*" (John 3:17).

God has brought more into my life than I ever could have imagined. No more hiding dark secrets, no more pretending, no more shame and hatred. He brought peace, love, and truth into my life. God's grace is the glue that holds my life together. He guides me through the heartache with His Word. He exposes the lies in my head with His truth. He calms my fears with His love. He wants to do the same for you. You are beloved by Him, the only One who will never leave your side.

When you pass through the waters,
I will be with you;
and when you pass through the rivers,
they will not sweep over you.
When you walk through the fire,
you will not be burned;
the flames will not set you ablaze.
For I am the LORD your God,
the Holy One of Israel, your Savior.

—Isaiah 43:2-3b

two

Changing the Lens

by Lily*

My dad was a preacher's son, my mom a gorgeous bad girl. They met in high school, and my mom made the first move. They had only been dating a short while when my mom found out she was pregnant with my sister. They quickly got married and my dad got busy making the money. He worked as a long-haul truck driver, which meant he was gone all week and only home on weekends.

When my sister was just three months old, my mom found out she was pregnant with none other than… me!

I grew up feeling as though my mom didn't like me or love me. I felt like a burden on her, and I believed that she didn't want me. Because of this, I always felt like an outsider in my own family, as though I needed to earn my place. I heard my mom fighting with my sister one day, and my mom said something along the lines of, "If you don't like my rules, then you can go live somewhere else."

That struck fear into my little-girl heart. I believed that if I ever screwed up, I'd get kicked out. I already had this complex that I wasn't liked, loved, or wanted, so when I heard that threat, it skewed the lens through which I saw myself in my family—the false lens through which I viewed the world—even further.

People have different lenses through which they view the world, that's why you can have fifty different interpretations of the same message preached in church. One person might feel guilty and condemned listening to a preacher preach, while the person sitting beside him feels loved and encouraged after hearing the same message. Some people have a victim mindset, or a victim lens through which they see the world. They believe that everyone is out to get them and all their problems are because of others. My lens was one of an orphan mindset; I did not believe I was loved and accepted unconditionally, that I was unlikable and therefore unlovable.

That mindset drove me to either avoid my mom so as not to anger her, or to go out of my way to do little tasks for her. Whenever my mom asked us to do something, I was always the first to volunteer. On one particular day, my mom called out, "Can someone get me a loaf of bread from the freezer?"

I was halfway out of my chair to go and get it when she followed up with, "And not Lily!" She said that as a courtesy to me, since I was always the one to do those tasks and she wanted to give me a break, but I found myself fighting back tears. Doing things for her was the only way I had to earn my place in the family, and that had been taken away from me.

Sometimes my dad would take my sisters and me on short trips in the truck with him. On one particular trip, I got to go with him all by myself, just me and my dad. You'd think that would be a dream come true for any kid, but I felt nervous and anxious the whole time. The thought that I didn't belong, that I hadn't earned my place, carried over from my home life to time spent with my father. I felt unworthy to be with him.

Can you see the pattern here? How my orphan mindset affected all areas of my life? It was as though I was wearing a pair of pink sunglasses—the lens didn't just affect the way I saw one thing, it affected how I saw everything.

Feeling unloved and unwanted followed me my whole life. As I got older, I started to wonder *why* I had always felt that way. I searched for some distinct memory that told me, this is it, this is the reason. And yes, there were painful memories, but nothing that felt traumatic enough to cause such strong feelings.

I couldn't make sense of it, especially since my parents had always told me they loved me. When my mom told me that, though, I honestly believed she was only saying she loved me out of duty. It's socially unacceptable to tell your child that you don't love them, even if you don't, so you say the words because it's the right thing to do. I actually believed that was what my mom thought.

My sisters did not have the same experience I did growing up. I talked with a couple of them about this and they said they always knew they were loved, even when things were bad at home, which they often were since the home I grew up in was a dysfunctional one. Even so, they knew they were loved.

In contrast, I distrusted people. I never allowed myself to be vulnerable with my friends. I wouldn't even open up to my best friend growing up. I tried hard to be a good listener and to be a friend others could trust, but I never trusted anyone enough to be transparent with them.

As a young woman, I became promiscuous. I craved the attention men gave me because it made me feel someone really wanted me; for a few fleeting moments I could believe that I was loved, even though I knew those guys didn't actually love me. It did briefly fulfill my need to be loved, but it was a horrible substitute for the real thing, because it left me feeling more unloved, and the giant hole in my heart only seemed to grow larger.

When I was twenty-two, I met the man who would become my husband. When we were dating, he pursued my heart. It took a lot of pursuing, because I didn't trust anyone and I opened up to no one. But this man saw me for who I truly was, not how others saw me, not how I saw myself. He saw me, as he put it, through God's eyes. And it was through that persistent love that I finally started to see myself through God's eyes too.

We married when I was twenty-five. The first couple of years were hard, mostly because of all my baggage. I had open, festering emotional wounds that caused me to strongly overreact when my husband would say or do something that touched one of those wounds. But even though those first couple of years were hard, they were still the best years of my life up to that point.

For the first time in my life, I *knew* I was loved. My wonderful husband proved that to me over and over again. I knew that no matter what I did or said, he loved me. I felt more fulfilled than I had ever felt before, even in the midst of all the fighting.

When you choose to see the gold instead of the dirt in someone, like my husband did, miracles happen.

Our second year of marriage we did the School of Biblical Studies with YWAM, a super-intensive course in which you basically write your own Bible commentary by the end of the year.

While there, I met a wonderful young woman named Sheila*, who asked me to hang out with her one day. I was very nervous because other women have always terrified me. As we walked and talked, I found myself warning her about me. I told her that people tend to be scared off and hurt by me because I'm straightforward and blunt. I was trying to push her away, like I had pushed all women away because I was so afraid of letting them get close to me and then being rejected. I was scared that they would see me for who I really was—this unlikable person with a terrible personality.

When I was a kid, my dad had told me that I was selfish and that was just part of my personality, part of who I was. I believed him. I thought that God had given me a selfish personality and there was nothing I could do about it. He also told me I was just like my mother, and I was pretty sure that neither my mom nor my dad liked who my mom was. If I was just like her then… well, you get the picture.

Sheila told me that God had pointed me out to her one day. God told her that I was on a journey of healing and He wanted her to walk alongside me. Sheila did indeed walk with me. She began pursuing my heart just like my husband had. What a beautiful picture of God's love for me—He kept sending people into my life who pursued my heart. People who dug deep, asked a lot of questions, and waited for me to answer.

Until that point in my life, I had never allowed myself to be

> What a beautiful picture of God's love for me–He kept sending people into my life who pursued my heart.

broken. My mom had gone through many painful experiences in her life, so any time I felt hurt growing up I shut down those feelings, reminding myself that they paled in comparison to hers. She was the one who had a reason to be hurt, not me.

Sheila asked wonderfully probing questions that got me to not only open up but also to see that I was indeed hurt and broken. That was the first step, acknowledging that I was broken. Over the next nine months or so, Sheila would schedule time with me on a regular basis. She always asked those deep questions, and I often felt like a million broken pieces lying in front of her. But what a wonderful thing it was to be broken with someone and to feel safe. With Sheila I didn't have to pretend everything was fine. I didn't have to have my guard up; all the defenses could come down.

That was a major turning point for me, because I learned that women don't have to be scary, and that it's good to open up and be vulnerable with people. After that I began seeking out mentors and counsellors. Those people didn't bring complete healing, but what they did do was help to reprogram my thinking about being transparent with people. I began to feel comfortable opening up and being vulnerable.

My husband and I had been home from Bible school for about a year when I got a call from my aunt. She said she had a family cookbook she wanted to give me, so I went to her place to pick it up. She asked me how my family was doing, and I shared with her that I hadn't seen my family in a while because I was taking a break from them to find inner healing.

As we talked further, she shared something with me that changed me forever. She said that my parents had planned on aborting me when they found out my mom was pregnant with me. My aunt brought this up innocently, because she'd been told that my mom had already revealed that truth to me. But my mother had never told me that; it was the first I had heard it.

As soon as she told me, I broke down crying. All those thoughts that had plagued me my whole life about feeling unloved and unwanted came flooding back into my mind. They taunted me saying, "See, see, you were never wanted. You were never loved, right from the start. It was all true."

But then something amazing happened. It was as though the voice of God pierced through all those dark voices and revealed them for what they truly were... lies. In that moment everything suddenly became clear—*this* was why I had always felt unloved and unwanted.

I did some research and found that it was a common phenomenon when a person's mother wanted an abortion but couldn't get one, or tried to abort the baby but failed, and the child was born alive, that person felt unloved and unwanted by his or her mother, even if she turned out to be a wonderful mother who loved her child.

I finally had my answer as to why I always felt unloved and unwanted. But the truth was that I had always been loved. Whether or not my mom had loved or wanted me, I was loved because God loved me. God wanted me. All of heaven celebrated the day of my birth... the day of my conception.

My mom loved me too, which is why she decided not to go through with the abortion, but even if she hadn't, no matter what the circumstances surrounding my conception and birth, I had always been loved and wanted.

If you are reading this and you have ever felt rejected and un-loved, I'm here to tell you that it's not true. If no one else was cele-brating your arrival into this world, God was, and all of heaven with Him. You are loved. You are wanted. You are valued.

Finding out about the intended abortion helped me to under-stand why my dad believed I had a selfish personality. When a child feels unloved, they basically go into survival mode. The child believes that no one has her back, so she must look after herself. A child can only give something if it has first been given to them.

Children who have not received love cannot give love, because they don't have it in them to give. The emotional and spiritual wounds I carried around had been incurred before I was even born, so I was in "survival mode" right from the start. It makes sense that my father thought selfishness was part of me. I was always looking out for myself and not others, since I believed no one was looking out for me.

If you are a mother and you considered aborting your child, I hope that my story doesn't make you feel ashamed. That is so not my intention in telling my story. You are forgiven, you are loved and accept-ed, and you can go boldly before Father God, unashamed. Father God loves you and *never* wants you to wallow in shame. If you've ever felt guilt or condemnation, please know that it was not Father God placing those feelings on you. He wants to set you free from those things.

You are loved, you are valuable, and you have great worth. No matter what happened in your past, you are worth the sacrifice of Jesus.

three

From a Mess to a Message

by Denise Mountenay

One night I was having a sleepover at my friend Diane's house. We decided to go play pool in the basement with her brother Jim, who was about twenty-four years old, and Rob, a nineteen year old who worked for Diane's father. I remember that "Bye, Bye, Miss American Pie" was playing on the radio. Her brother and Rob were pros as they made almost every shot. However, Diane and I were horrible amateurs, and rarely got a ball in the hole… although we laughed and giggled and made fun of our fluke shots. The guys had a few beers and Jim kept eye-balling me. Every time he did, I looked away.

It was getting late, and I was so exhausted, so I said, "Hey Diane, let's go call Steve." And we ran upstairs giggling. After phoning Steve, a classmate, and taking turns asking him silly questions, we hung up. We changed into our nightgowns, and Diane told me she was going to go give Rob a kiss goodnight. I got into bed, pulled the covers up, turned onto my side, and started to drift off to sleep.

The creak of the bedroom door opening woke me up. I blinked, confused. Where was I? Everything was so dark. And then I saw the outline of a naked man. Before I could move, or cry out, he pulled up my nightgown and was on top of me. Diane's brother had snuck into the room and was raping me. I struggled to try to get him off of me and move away, but he was much heavier and stronger than me. I was so surprised and afraid, and the experience was horrible. As I cried and groaned, he held his hand tightly over my mouth and told me to, "Shut up, and be still." When he had finished and left, I lay there, shocked and in pain.

I felt too ashamed and defiled to tell anyone what had happened, so sadly, like most rape victims, I kept silent.

I was only thirteen years old, and he had stolen my virginity.

Tragically, my story is typical for a lot of girls and boys in this generation. I grew up with a very liberal Swiss mother, and my father was a hard-core German atheist. At the age of sixteen, I had my first crush. I was so infatuated with Terry. We had gone out for several months and had been sleeping together. I believe I thought, on a subconscious level, that since I was not a virgin anymore, what was the difference?

One day, suddenly and without warning, Terry decided to break up with me because he wanted to go out with someone else. I was heartbroken. My mom encouraged me to take a trip to Switzerland to work in my aunt's restaurant and learn some Swiss-German. The idea of getting away for a while was appealing, so I went.

My aunt was about eight months pregnant with her first child when I arrived. She was so excited. I wasn't there long before I started feeling nauseated and began vomiting in the mornings, so my aunt sent me to the doctor for a checkup. I sat on the hard table in a room where everything was stark, cold, and white, waiting for the doctor to return. His words, when he came back, felt as stark and cold as the room. "You are going to have a baby," he reported in his strong German accent.

I left the clinic in a daze and took a long walk up a mountain road, tears streaming down my face. What should I do? How would I tell my parents? I walked for a long time, and gradually my resolve strengthened. I could do this. I would work in my aunt's restaurant as long as I could, saving every penny. And I might be able to sneak some of her baby clothes too, since she had bought and been given so many outfits as gifts. Surely she wouldn't miss a few items if I took them and hid them away. Now I just needed to figure out how to tell my parents the news in a letter.

A few days later, I was driving my grandfather's moped and went around a sharp corner, lost control, and hit a van head on. With no helmet, I was thrown hard onto the road. The moped was a write-off, but somehow I walked away without even a scratch. Upset and crying, I called my mom and told her about the accident, assuring her that I was okay. She caught the next flight to Zurich and showed up at my aunt's home the next day.

When I told her I was pregnant, she put her arm around me and said, "Denise, love, you are only sixteen, you have your whole life ahead of you. Come back home with me. You can just have this operation, and you won't be pregnant anymore."

I figured that if it was okay with my mom, and it was okay with the doctors and the government, then it must be okay.

As soon as I got home, I called Terry to tell him I was pregnant. He totally denied that he could have gotten me pregnant as he had a prostate problem. I had no idea what that was, but told him he was the only man I had been with the last few months. I did assure him that he didn't have to worry, as my mom had made an appointment for me to have this operation so I wouldn't be pregnant anymore. He was glad to hear that, and I ended the call.

No one gave me information about what an abortion is, or told me how far along I was, or at what stage of development the baby was. I went into the procedure kind of like a sheep being led to slaughter.

My mom took me to the hospital where they put me to sleep and killed my first child. My mom told me to forget about it and get on with my life. In my case, that meant drinking more and starting to do drugs. Under the influence, I became more promiscuous. Deep down, though, the only thing I really wanted was to meet a nice guy, get married, and have a family.

At the age of twenty-six, I was living in Toronto and working as a successful multi-line insurance agent when I found out I was pregnant a second time. Tim, a computer genius, and I had been going out for a few months, we got along very well, and I thought maybe he was the one I would marry one day. However, he wasn't as serious.

At the doctor's office, I again found myself sitting in a small, sterile room with the doctor who had just given me the news. I pressed a hand to my stomach. "How far along am I?"

He glanced at my file. "About eight or nine weeks."

This time, I was determined to know more before I made any decisions. "What has developed so far?"

The doctor reached for a blank piece of paper and used a pen to draw a tiny dot. "Basically it is nothing at this point, just a clump of tissue."

I didn't realize it at the time, but he was outright lying to me. He told me to tell the receptionist to make an appointment for me at the Buffalo Clinic as it could be done much faster there. So I followed my doctor's orders. Years later I discovered the truth and was devastated to learn the facts about the humanity of children in utero, and how abortions were such a brutal, barbaric form of birth control.

When I told Tim I was pregnant, he went into a fit of rage and demanded I have an abortion. He kicked me out of his house and said he never wanted to see me again. Heavy-hearted, I left.

Alone once more, and with no support, I couldn't see any other options. I called my friend Stacey to come with me to the abortion mill in Buffalo, NY, so she could drive me home afterwards. That horrific event will always be etched in my memory. Inside the abortion clinic were many pregnant women like me. We delved into the *Cosmopolitan* and *People* magazines in the reception area, trying not to think about why we were there. A clinic worker called my name, and I followed her into another little room where she asked me a few questions such as whether or not I had any allergies and then asked if I knew why I was there.

"Yeah," I answered. She had me sign some papers and told me to go and put on the gown she'd laid out in a tiny change room. When I finished, she led me down a long corridor into another little room with three or four other women. I was nervous, mostly numb, just going through the motions, cold and detached. Again, no one gave me any information whatsoever about the risks of abortion, or about my baby, nor did they let me know that I had any other options. All they did was tell me to follow them wherever they were going.

An abortion worker came into this room and asked if anyone wanted any Tylenol. I said, "Yeah, I'll take two bottles." She laughed and gave me two pills in a little plastic cup with some water. My turn came, and I was led into the operating room. After I lay down on the cold table, covered with a thin strip of paper, I was told to put my legs up on the stirrups. It was quite uncomfortable and embarrassing. The abortionist said I was about ten weeks along, and he began to force my cervix open with various cold steel gadgets. Then he turned on this machine and began the procedure.

Immediately, the pain was excruciating. I screamed in agony and cried out, "Stop it, Stop it!"

He said, "No," and kept on doing it. I felt as though I was being raped again, but much worse. That is how horrible abortion feels.

When it was over, they slapped a pad between my legs; there was a lot of blood. I curled into a fetal position, feeling as though my brain had snapped. After a few minutes, the clinic worker came in and told me to hurry up as other women were waiting. But I was in some kind of shock. I couldn't talk—I could barely move.

It's clear why they had such a long corridor between the reception area and the room where the abortions were taking place. No one involved with the abortions would want the people in the waiting room to hear the screams and cries of the women going through this horrific ordeal.

Immediately after my second abortion, I took a leave of absence from my successful insurance career. I was an emotional mess. Soon I discovered I had contracted an infection from the procedure, and who knows what other damage. The experience was so traumatizing, I wanted to die. I sank into a deep depression, isolated myself, booked myself into the YWCA, and drank and drank and did drugs.

After several months, my concerned mother called one of my girlfriends and asked her to go and see how I was doing. My friend made me go out with her to a bar where we drank and got stoned. A handsome guy picked me up, and we had a one-night stand. I got pregnant a third time.

You are probably wondering how a woman in this day and age, with all the birth control out there, could get pregnant. Well, I had been on the Pill, and it gave me bad side effects. An IUD landed me in a hospital, and the men I was with didn't want to wear condoms.

The shame of not knowing this guy's last name was enough for me to decide to have a third abortion. However, I wanted to be asleep when they did it—I never wanted to go through the pain of an abortion wide awake again—so I booked an appointment at a hospital in Toronto. I had bought into the lie, told to me repeatedly, that the baby inside me was not really a baby but merely a clump of tissue. The doctors and everyone else I spoke to seemed to think it was okay to have an abortion as a solution to my unplanned pregnancies. Not once did anyone offer help or support for me as a mother, or tell me the truth about fetal development.

Not long after this third abortion, I began to contemplate the big picture of the world. My teachers had taught me the theory of evolution when I went to school, including the idea that human beings evolved from apes. However, when I really began to think about it, I realized that every living creature reproduces its own kind. Whales have baby whales, giraffes have baby giraffes, eagles have baby eagles, monkeys have baby monkeys, and sheep have baby sheep. And there are huge missing links between animals and people.

That raised questions in my mind. Is there a God? Who is God? Which way to God was the right way? And I began to investigate the major world religions to find out what each taught and believed. As I studied each one, something always seemed awry. At the age of thirty, I surrendered my life to the Lord Jesus Christ. While at a Women's Aglow Conference in Beaverton, Ontario, I received the revelation that abortion had killed my children. They were not just "clumps of tissue", but children created in the image of God.

With deep sorrow, remorse, and regret, I cried out to God for forgiveness. With loud wailing and repentance, I grieved for the loss of my children. They were my babies.

My favourite song is "Amazing Grace" because the grace that saved a wretch like me is truly amazing. That I would be forgiven for my ignorance and stupid decisions to go along with abortions is almost more than I can comprehend. That Jesus Christ died on the cross and paid the penalty even for the sin of having my children murdered is the truth that counteracts all the lies I have ever been told.

A huge weight had been lifted off me, and soon the Holy Spirit began to work in me, calling me to speak out and be a voice for my children who'd had no voice. The first few times I spoke in our young adults Bible study group, I could only cry. But slowly, as I persevered with determination and God's help, He gave me the courage and boldness to share my testimony on the pain and damage of legal abortion and how it had taken the lives of my children.

When I learned the truth about fetal development and discovered the amazing scientific facts about DNA, I was blown away. Wrap your mind around this: all the knowledge about how a human will develop eyes to see, ears to hear, a mouth, teeth, all vital organs with their unique and distinct function, hair in all the right places, everything was there from the moment of conception! The heart begins to work and beat a mere three weeks after fertilization. We have arms, legs, fingers, and toes by eight to nine weeks gestation. This process does not take millions of years, but days, weeks, and months.

Abortion had caused extensive damage to my cervix/uterus and I had to have two lumps removed from my left breast too. When I began to study the complications of legal abortion, I discovered there are many studies linking breast cancer to induced abortion. This does not mean that every woman who has had an abortion will get breast cancer, but the risk does go up.

Abortion is the greatest crime against humanity in our days. This practice of dismembering and/or poisoning children alive in their mother's womb breaks the heart of God. He has opened many doors for me to share my testimony and teach on the damage and danger of abortion and bring humanity to children in utero.

Over the last fifteen years, the Lord has sent me into the United Nations (UN) where I have brought teams and conducted side events at the Commission on the Status of Women in New York. I have also spoken at the UN Headquarters in Geneva, Switzerland, during the World Health Organization Assembly for several years now, and I meet with UN ambassadors and delegates on this critical human rights issue. God has sent me to many nations and into universities, conferences, and different denominations with this truth and message for such a time as this.

About thirty-one years ago, Jesus appeared to me in my Toronto apartment with my three aborted children in front of Him. They were as old when I saw them as they would have been if they had lived, and I somehow knew their names. Jennifer would have been about sixteen or seventeen at the time, and she looked so much like me. Daniel was about six or seven, and Rebecca five or six. They were beautiful children!

With tears in my eyes, I asked each one to forgive me, and each child said they did. When I was wiping away my tears, they all disappeared. I know they are with the Lord in heaven, and I will see them again one day. But they were never given the opportunity to fulfill the plans God had for them on the earth.

In Canada, we pay for over 100,000 children to be brutally killed before birth every year with our money and silence. Their blood cries out for justice. The mothers and fathers of aborted children need to know they can be forgiven and set free through the precious blood of Jesus Christ (Yeshua).

> Followers of Christ must be a voice for the voiceless–if we aren't, who will be?

God wants us to be the salt and light of the earth. It is time for the church to repent for her apathy and complacency regarding this diabolical practice in our cities and nations. Followers of Christ must be a voice for the voiceless—if we aren't, who will be? We defeat Satan by the blood of the Lamb and the word of our testimony, as confirmed in Revelation 12:11, Proverbs 31:8, Ephesians 5:11, and Revelation 21:8.

Please pray for me as I am on the frontlines of this war on pregnant women and their children. For more information on my work and ministry, visit www.togetherforlife.net.

May God give us all the courage we need to stand up and say "No more."

four

Every Good and Perfect Gift

by Jared Hathaway

If I want to do this story justice, to give God the glory He deserves, I have to go back. Way, way back. My dear mother and father showed us kids what faith in the giver of every good and perfect gift looked like long before any of us even came to be, and I'm grateful that they've occasionally recounted that story for our benefit.

Mom had cysts on her ovaries when she was only twelve years old. The decision was made to operate, and the doctors removed one ovary completely and half of the other one. She was told that it was very likely that she would be infertile. She came from a family with five kids, and Dad had three siblings and ten aunts and uncles on his father's side alone. So large families were kind of a big deal.

Of course, Mom let Dad know about her medical history while they were dating (or "courting" as they called it—so old fashioned). Dad said that he didn't think it would be right to allow that to halt their relationship. I believe he saw this as an opportunity to trust the Lord to provide according to His will, to exercise faith in the same God who had "opened the wombs" of many women in the Bible— Sarah and Rachel and Elizabeth, to name a few.

Well, God certainly did reward them, because not only did Mom have *a* baby, she had five babies (and was only pregnant four times). I guess doctors aren't always right, huh?

Okay, let's fast forward some decades. My wife and I had been married about five years and had recently moved into a beautiful home, as we were both making decent money. We decided that if we waited until we were "ready," we might never be parents. So now seemed like the right time. And wouldn't you know it, only a couple months later she took the test and it worked! I was gonna be a daddy. Oh boy. Wow.

We went in for an ultrasound. I think we both cried when we saw that little, rapid, open-close-open-close video representation of our baby's heartbeat on the screen. The world kind of stands still in moments like that, because you're staring at evidence that life is gonna dramatically change. *Has* changed, actually. I was so excited. I even went on Facebook to announce that this wasn't a drill. That a baby was on the way.

And then, the worst day of our lives happened. During the next scheduled appointment, the baby's heartbeat couldn't be detected. Six weeks along and then no more. Devastation. My wife miscarried at home a few days later, days in which I had prayed in earnest for a miracle that didn't come. I was there. We were traumatized together.

A dark few months followed. Afterwards came a pretty dark year. But slowly we moved along with life. If we had been careful not to get pregnant before, she was doubly careful not to let it happen again. And that crushed me all over, because I still held onto hope. I knew the value of a family. I wanted to start and lead my own. But then my dad's words came back to me, how he had faced the decision whether to marry my mom or not. He'd said that he was determined that if we kids couldn't come naturally to them, they'd be open to adoption. Those words gave me renewed hope.

So in 2014 we became licensed to provide foster care to children in Franklin County. What an eye-opening and amazing experience that was. We had more than thirty kids come through our home in only six months, sometimes for a couple of nights, others for longer. While it was exceedingly difficult, it was some of the most rewarding work I've ever done.

And then—I marvel now at God's providence—a cute little blonde-haired girl was placed onto "the list." She was only sixteen months old, and parental rights had been terminated. She was a ward of the state, and her foster mom wouldn't be seeking to adopt her. That was a rarity. We thought, sure, why not throw our names into the hopper with the fifty (fifty!) other families who'd made a direct appeal to add her to theirs.

She was a failure-to-thrive case. Mother had abused drugs and alcohol throughout pregnancy and after, making no attempt to follow a mandated plan of reconciliation. The poor baby was born weighing six pounds and only weighed 6.1 pounds at her three-month check-up. The state of Ohio moved in, saving her precious life, thank God. By now she was healthy, having been in foster care for over four hundred days. You dare not get your hopes too far up, because two percent chance means ninety-eight percent chance they'll pick someone else—people who have fostered for years and years.

Lo and behold, *we* were chosen! No joke, they loved us and thought we would be an excellent placement. I agreed, of course, but what an unexpected blessing. And then, get this, we looked at this little girl's birth date—March 28, 2013. We'd had the miscarriage on the 23rd. Can you believe that?!

While we were in pieces, our lives shattered by loss, God was at work behind the scenes, picking up those broken pieces and mending them without our knowledge or permission. What victory! What amazing Grace! What mighty providence!

Raelen came to live in our home on my birthday in 2014, and called me Mommy for about three months, because the foster home had no man in it.

Ahem.

Our family was small but perfect, just the three of us. Raelen began to say "Daddy" and to associate it with me around the first of the year in 2015. We decided to take a respite from fostering kids to kind of establish the family identity, ya know?

But then we started getting the itch again, and the agency continued to call us because our license was still active. We took in a couple of older teenage girls for a few months, then one fateful day we got a call—a newborn needed a place to stay.

Baby had a few health issues, mainly withdrawals from the pain-killers Mother had been on. (And by the way, it's incredibly heart-breaking to watch such a tiny baby fighting the symptoms.)

The baby's name was Sade. We had actually prayed for a new-born so we could say we'd had the experience, but we did need to consider that we had a two year old to take care of at the time. In the end, though, we couldn't say no and agreed to take the plunge.

Pretty incredible—the sleepless nights and formula and teeny tiny diapers and the crying and the major adjustments, all worth it times ten, if I had to assess it. We did meet the bio parents, in case you were wondering. In fact, we practically became foster parents to the parents too. They were actually good people, but addicted to the things I was taught to "just say no" to and have.

They were multi-generational poverty cases and pretty much caught in a rough rut, a cyclical maelstrom of dependency and un-employment. But they were making strides and shaping up. They passed drug tests almost immediately after their baby was taken, and continued in that course of victory. It was impressive.

Then came a night I'll never forget. We'd had our weekly visit with them a day or two before. The poor guy called me up almost in tears, not knowing what to do or where to turn. (I look back now with 20/20, understanding why it was that he trusted us and had the boldness to reach out, and how horrible it might have been if Christ had not been so evident in our lives.)

"Ya gotta help me," he said.

Naturally, I said that I'd help in any way I could.

"We're gonna need a ride to Cleveland. We ain't got a car. Our daughter needs to go to the hospital."

"All right. Why?"

After a bit of probing on my part, he finally blurted it out. "My son has messed up bad. He got with my wife's daughter. She's five months pregnant. She's only twelve. Now I have to send my son back to Pennsylvania. There's an abortion clinic that will do late terms in Cleveland. We ain't ready to be grandparents. Can you please give us a ride?"

My God in *heaven*.

Well, no, there would be no ride to Cleveland. I hung up after I told him I would call back in a couple minutes. In a brief, but very intense conversation, my wife and I concluded that this was a literal life-and-death situation—that we'd been presented with an opportunity that certainly could have eternal consequences. I called the man back.

"No, we cannot violate our consciences and provide what you're asking. But here's what we *can* and *will* do. We are going to help your daughter in any and every possible way. She will have this baby in four months. And if it's determined that she is able to raise the baby in your household, we will celebrate that with you. If you think that this child would be better in the loving home of adopted parents, we will help that come to pass. Or if you, your wife, and your daughter believe that my family, the one that has your baby right now, would make a fitting family for him or her, we would be open to that route."

"Really?"

The forty-three-year-old pending grandfather sounded a little shocked. His wife, about to become a grandmother, was younger than my wife.

"Absolutely."

The rest is kind of history. We had to keep everything secret until Ella was born, because the birth mother can and sometimes does change her mind. In the meantime, Sade was reunited with them. A successful and happy case study in foster care services.

We offered open adoption, but they were content to basically put things behind them and move back to Philadelphia. The girl never really acknowledged that she was pregnant. Didn't register, you know? Asked how the baby was gonna come out.

> God makes no errors. He has ordered our footsteps and provided us with a sacrificial example, that He may be glorified in the faithful living out of our lives.

It was a caesarean delivery. The hospital staff was amazing, treating us as the parents to this newborn that we were about to be.

These experiences have changed the perspective I now have on life, on love, and on the power of words. But mostly on what God can and will do in the lives of people who are simply willing to be obedient to their calling.

Ella, the baby that almost wasn't born, played baby Jesus in my church's Christmas play three months later.

God makes no errors. He has ordered our footsteps and provided us with a sacrificial example, that He may be glorified in the faithful living out of our lives.

As the Apostle Paul wrote in Galatians 2:20a, "… *I no longer live, but Christ lives in me.*"

five

What Hope Looks Like

by Felicia Simard

When I was younger, I believed that abortion was a form of birth control. Of course, as a child I believed many things, such as daily police visits were common for all families due to drug, alcohol, and physical abuse between parents. By the time I was ten years old, I believed—in fact I knew—that I no longer wanted to live in a house with strange men sleeping on our couches.

I had been born into an addicted family. Crack cocaine and alcohol were my parents' choices of toxins and poisons. As you can imagine, it was a very dysfunctional home that included incest and molestation by drug dealers.

Even at a young age, I decided I no longer wanted to be a victim of those broken men who seemed to sexually gravitate towards children. And I understood that what my brother was doing by joining in was not normal either.

By the time I was eleven, you'd be looking at a girl who smoked cigarettes daily and who would lose her virginity at thirteen to one of her mother's crack cocaine dealers. A dealer who was later shot in the chest with a shotgun and pronounced dead at the scene.

For a long time, I thought I was untouchable, a rebellious, reckless child. I was a liar, manipulator, and depressed. I hated everyone and trusted no one, especially myself.

I was suicidal, and I hated my gender because, in my world, it felt as though it rendered me powerless. In 2005, my family got shot at and we ended up in the witness protection program.

When I was sixteen, I was told to drop out of high school to help support the family. At eighteen, I was kicked out of my home and homeless because the government stopped issuing the baby bonus at that age and I was no longer their paycheck.

So, an extremely abusive man who had once handcuffed me in his mother's basement offered me "shelter."

By twenty-one, I had lived in nineteen different apartments, in parks, on benches, and in cars, centres, and shelters. Perhaps inevitably, in my quest for survival, I landed myself a one-way ticket to the Vanier women's correctional facility.

I had no hope because I had no idea what hope even looked like. Then I found myself pregnant and holding the weight of the world in a tiny ultrasound.

At the top of the ultrasound picture, it said *Felicia Simard*, which made it all very real. It wasn't the first time I had been here.

Maybe because I'd believed what society said about abortion being a form of birth control, or maybe, even more, because I was terrified of being found out, I had chosen to end that pregnancy. I wish I'd had more hope for that one.

But this one. At twenty-one, I was holding her. Literally and figuratively, that black and white photograph showed me, for the first time in a long time—maybe ever—what hope really looked like.

I was homeless. I was a high-functioning drug addict, weekend cocaine addict, alcoholic, and I was pregnant. So why did I choose life? Because I found a resource. Another way. A place of safety. Something tangible to help support my new walk, my new journey. A not-so-local maternity home.

Before I entered the home of W.I.N.G.S. (Wait, Invest, Nurture, Grow, Soar) Maternity, I was a negative atheist. I knew it was a requirement to go to church if I wanted to stay there, but I didn't mind because I'd attended Catholic school and simply wanted a bed to sleep in instead of floors and cars.

Two short years later, that home and Jesus made a believer out of me.

I accepted Christ into my life, not because of a religious establishment or Sunday services, although those were becoming more and more enjoyable with time, but because I saw Marion Cozens, the mother hen and owner of the home walking the walk. She didn't just talk about Jesus or act hypocritical. She wasn't perfect, nor did she pretend to be. I respected that she was human in every way but still lived out her Christian faith in a way I'd never witnessed before.

I felt the love immediately when I walked through the doors. Many of the girls complained about the daily programs in the home such as pre-natal, cooking, school, inner healing, art therapy, and counselling, but personally I was thankful for a safe place to rest my head and structure. I thrived on structure, in fact, and have needed to create it many times because of the organized chaos in my life, so it was nice to not be the self-delegator for this part of my life.

We ran as a family, and just like families we bumped heads many times, but we also shared moments and memories together as a unit. We went on special outings and events like Great Wolf Lodge and Medieval Times, places I would never have been able to go to without the support and community surrounding W.I.N.G.S. Maternity.

Living with three to four other moms at a time was often a challenge as we were indeed all very pregnant and all very hormonal women, but I gained a sisterhood, if even for a time, and found it helpful to have the others in my life as we walked with each other through our new mama journeys.

Before this home, I wasn't sure how being a mom was even feasible for me. All I knew was that I needed to care for my babe on the way emotionally, spiritually, financially, and morally the way I needed to be cared for when I was a child. Unfortunately, I had no idea where to start or what that would even look like. W.I.N.G.S. taught me how to begin to be a mom, giving me the practical and spiritual tools that I needed. Tools of hope. Tools I needed to believe I could really do it.

Even after the birth of my daughter, this home gave me a community of people to help support my daughter and me in the process of becoming a family. It was a stepping stone into what I now feel called to do.

The support I found at the maternity home offered me another option when I found out I was pregnant. That option was to choose life! And when I chose life for my unborn child, my own life began.

Since the birth of my beautiful girl, I have travelled to assemblies all across Ontario sharing my absolute nothing-to-something glory story to show others that God really does resurrect us out of our ashes and makes us into something beautiful.

Getting off drugs, finding a home, and walking away from my choice of toxic liquids sober was a miracle. Maybe I could have done those things myself, given enough time and support. But God, only God, could, in four short years, do all that while elevating me to a place of forgiveness and healing. A place that changed the way I speak to myself as well as others, how I interact with people and give back to society.

He opened doors for me to pursue higher education by completing seminary courses and working towards a Bachelor's degree in theology.

God transformed my mind and enabled me to safely deliver a beautiful seven-pound, two-ounce baby girl into this world, changing mine forever. And He brought it all together by gifting us with a heaven-sent father figure and man who brought redemption to mankind, including me and my tiny-yet-mighty family.

With the Word of God as my coach, I have emerged from the empty shell of myself to a place of transparency in sharing my story with organizations, charities, non-profits, assemblies, churches, newspapers, local television networks, and, most excitedly, at the feet of Parliament Hill. And now I am sharing it with you.

I have been the face on brochures for religious organizations, pro-life organizations, and maternity homes. I've been featured in local and not-so-local newspapers, in articles and websites, as a guest blogger on on-the-rise social media platforms, and had pieces of my story told on global television.

From the feedback I have received, my story has had an impact on hearts. It has changed lives. And only God could do that. He is the God of acceleration, of redemption, of healing, of elevation. By most standards, I should never have had this beautiful child. Many would argue that, since I did not appear to be in a position to support her or give her the stable home she needed, I should have simply ended her life. But God. God created my child and has a plan for her life. Why would He not then enable me to take care of her?

> But God. God created my child and has a plan for her life. Why would He not then enable me to take care of her?

I want to encourage anyone who may be facing an unplanned pregnancy, whether you are religious or not—since unplanned pregnancies do not discriminate—or if you know someone who is. If I could, in the most vulnerable and broken state imaginable, choose life and come out on the other side, not just surviving but thriving, then anyone facing an unplanned pregnancy is capable of being not just brave enough but strong enough to choose life.

Support and resources are available—grab them. I didn't have any idea what kind of help was available until I found myself in a situation where I desperately needed it. And that's why I have such a passion to be an ambassador for pro-life issues in Canada. Help is available. Options exist. Organizations such as Choice42 have championed me and repeatedly given me a platform to share my story. Our hope is that others like me will find the substantial support and information needed to navigate through other options for Mom and baby so that the pregnancy, even an unplanned one, doesn't end in abortion.

In Revelation 12:11, it says, *"They triumphed over him by the blood of the Lamb, and by the word of their testimony…"*

Satan desires death, but God brings life. And death is defeated when we share our stories, when we testify what God has done, and when we show love and support for those struggling with the decision of whether or not to have an abortion. May God use my story to show each of those women that they are loved, their babies are loved, and there is help and support available for them so that they can choose life.

six

A Life Worth Fighting For

by Julia Matveyeva

I will start my story by bringing you back in history to April 26, 1986, when the world's worst nuclear accident to date occurred at the Chernobyl nuclear plant near Kiev in Ukraine. A flawed reactor designed at the Chernobyl Nuclear Power Plant No.4 caused an explosion, which spewed radiation into the air. Before engineers and scientists could get it under control, 190 tons of highly radioactive materials were released into the atmosphere. The radioactive particles rained down not only on Chernobyl, but all over Ukraine, as well as the neighbouring countries of Belarus and Russia, and continued to drift over to other European countries. Scientists estimate that the amount of particles released was equivalent to the effect of twenty nuclear bombs. The Chernobyl accident remains the largest peacetime nuclear disaster ever.

This memorable event has also been marked on the calendar of our family.

Since my dad was military personnel back then, he was called upon as one of the liquidators to deal with the consequences of the nuclear explosion and to help evacuate citizens from the contaminated areas. He risked everything, and so did thousands of workers who came to that exclusion zone.

When my dad returned home after his service in Chernobyl, he tried to lead a normal life, helping my mother raise their newborn son and attempting to move past all the terrible moments he'd had to experience. He was regularly checked in hospitals and eventually health problems medically linked to radiation exposure were discovered. Unfortunately, he had a weakened immune system and struggled with the psychological trauma he'd endured as the liquidator in the contamination zone.

In 1989, my mom got pregnant. About six or seven weeks into her pregnancy, they were forced to move to another city, from Chernigov to Krivoy Rog, in Ukraine. As they settled in, my mom went to the hospital to be registered and checked by a gynecologist. When the doctors found out that my mom's husband had been a liquidator at Chernobyl, they strongly recommended she get an immediate abortion due to the high risk of developing what was likely a deformed fetus and giving birth to a child who could very well have serious disabilities.

After the radioactive fallout, many children were born with severe birth defects, so tens of thousands of women chose to end their pregnancies with abortions—some on the advice of their doctors and some in spite of it. These choices are reflected in the birth rate data from that part of the world in 1986 and 1988. Within Soviet Ukraine, thousands more women requested abortions in the months after the disaster, compared to the baseline rate. That period of time was infused with a profound sense of sorrow, which infiltrated people's lives as insidiously as the radioactive particles penetrated their bodies. Many families may not have been psychologically prepared to continue pregnancies, even without the threat of birth defects.

So, the doctors kept urging my mom to get rid of the baby, now eight weeks along, warning her of, as they said, "the inevitable consequences of raising a disabled/crippled child and hating your life for it." It was a tough time for my mom, having to resist the pressure coming from everywhere, yet she refused to undergo an abortion. So, the doctors had my mom fill out a special form where she had to pledge that if the baby was born with serious health complications, as they had warned her, she wouldn't abandon it by giving it to the orphanage for disabled children. It wasn't an easy decision for her to make as she'd heard many frightening stories about women giving birth to babies with congenital abnormalities.

Still, my mom claimed, "I didn't have any fear or doubt about keeping my baby. My child will be completely healthy, I just know it!" What a brave woman she is. As she had lots of check-ups at the hospital during her pregnancy period, she tried to stay strong and remain calm and hold on to her belief in a miracle. Surprisingly enough, all her tests showed normal results regarding the development of the baby in her womb. And when my mom gave birth, all the doctors were astonished. After checking the baby, they reported that she was completely healthy, which was an extremely rare case. The doctors said it was a "mere miracle."

> I know that God had a plan when He made me and placed me into my mother's womb. And He has a plan for your life too.

That baby girl was me.

I am grateful to my mom for believing the impossible and allowing me to be born a living miracle.

My mom and dad were so happy about their decision to keep the baby and raise their voices against abortion.

I know that God had a plan when He made me and placed me into my mother's womb. And He has a plan for your life too.

"For you created my inmost being; you knit me together in my mother's womb. I praise you because I am fearfully and wonderfully made; your works are wonderful, I know that full well" (Psalm 139:13-14).

seven

Finding Joy

A Grieving Grandma's Story

I dared not ask her anything. I noticed a tiny bump in her tummy as she stood at the kitchen sink, but I didn't want my daughter to think I was hinting that she was getting fat. She was at that stage where she and many of her friends were struggling with body image. I bit my tongue and didn't judge. Now I know—that bump was my grandchild. My grandchild! Oh, if I had only known.

My daughter shot a glance at me and our eyes met briefly. That glance now haunts me. It was one of appeal. As if she was saying, *Mom, don't you know? I want you to know, but I don't want to tell you. I want you to understand the conflict in me right now, but I dare not tell you.*

I'd been having dreams at this time. Two vivid dreams that I now also look back on and wonder if God was trying to tell me something. In fact, I question how I could even have dreams like these. Was my heart picking up on something and trying to tell my mind, or at least my spirit?

In my first dream, I held a test tube into which a baby had been squished. I immersed the test tube in milk. After a few days I took her out, but she had suffocated because of being in the milk too long. I tried to shake her out and get her back into shape while crying out to God to give her back life, but she was gone. In the dream, I knew in my heart I could have saved her if I had taken her out sooner, when she was still breathing. But it was too late now—she was gone forever.

The second dream was similar in that I was trying desperately to hold on to my baby boy while travelling in a car. But the road was steep, and I couldn't hold on to him. A woman offered to hold him for me, and then ate him. Doctors said they would give the lady medicine to help her give me back my baby. But there was something sinister about this lady—she cast a spell on the doctors and they were unable to make the medicine. So I couldn't get my baby back. He was gone.

Strange dreams, I know, but both of them showed babies who were alive then something happened and they died. I wailed and wailed in my dreams, begging God to bring them back to life. I know now that when I had these dreams my daughter was six weeks pregnant, but I didn't have any clue at the time.

Our kids went to spend the holidays with their grandparents. When I spoke to my mother, she mentioned that our daughter was sleeping a lot and wondered what was wrong with her. Before leaving, our daughter had been to the doctor and had given us an excuse for that visit, so we put her fatigue down to whatever that was. Or maybe she was being a typical teenager who likes to sleep in.

Of course, we now know she was visiting the doctor because she was pregnant, and the tiredness was a result of that. But when you don't suspect something, you don't see all the clues.

It was a hectic, stressful time for us, and it's hard in those kinds of times to do anything but simply try to cope. A friend who had noticed that our daughter was extra tired actually asked me if she could possibly be pregnant. I thought that was a ridiculous idea, but I asked my daughter anyway. She told me she was waiting for marriage, so I left it at that.

Oh, why didn't I press further and bring the truth out into the open before the baby died? Why didn't my dreams speak to me louder or more clearly? How had I missed this moment? Opportunity presented itself. But opportunity was lost and gone forever. Irreversible. A life destroyed.

Our kids came back after their time away with photos of themselves with my parents. I look at those photos now and think about how they are the only photos I have of my parents with a great-grandchild of theirs. Hidden inside our daughter's tummy, but nonetheless there in the photo with them. My parents didn't live to see the children that were eventually born to our kids, so that was the only time they "met" a great-grandchild. The photos sadden yet comfort me at the same time.

A few weeks later I saw a lot of blood in the main bathroom toilet. I assumed our daughter's period must have been heavy that month. I had no clue about the devastating situation she had been in, and what the blood was really from. Yes, from her abortion. From the loss of her child. My grandchild! The aftermath of the destruction of our grandchild.

It had taken my mother a long time to get pregnant with me. After I was born, she miscarried her second child, which she blamed herself for because someone came knocking at the door of their B & B, and she took them in despite how tired she was feeling. She told me how much she had cried at the loss. My father recounted that the doctor had handed him the baby, which was perfectly formed, and told him to put his son in the garbage. My parents did go on to have another child, but I have often wondered about my brother in Heaven.

I struggled to get pregnant too. Each month felt like a miscarriage when I was hoping so hard to be pregnant but found out I wasn't. I always longed to have lots of children and grandchildren. Being able to have the children we do have is a blessing that I count every day. As it says in Proverbs 23:18, *"There is surely a future hope for you, and your hope will not be cut off."*

I remember vividly the day, three months after seeing that blood in the bathroom, that our daughter came down the stairs in our home, her eyes teary. I asked her what was wrong, and she told me she had been raped. I hugged her tightly and tried to console her as she sobbed in my arms. I asked her if she had gotten pregnant or was worried about any diseases. At first she said she had thought she was pregnant but she wasn't. As we talked, though, she ended up telling me that she'd had an abortion. The pressure on her from society was so great that she felt she couldn't possibly keep her baby. She also believed she wasn't capable of having a child that would remind her of the rape.

She wanted to go to court and charge the guy who had raped her. We did go, but unfortunately it is incredibly difficult to bring about a conviction. Since there were no witnesses, it was his word against hers. The man went free. Our daughter kept crying, "It's not fair, it's not fair." Another wound for her to bury deep within her soul.

I cried, I wailed. I wailed, I howled. I couldn't stop crying for days on end after finding out about the abortion. I was paralyzed with grief. I didn't want to eat. I only wanted my grandchild. I pondered the tiny baby. *What colour hair do you have? Are you a boy or a girl? What do you like or dislike?* I wanted to reverse time, to go back to the weeks when my daughter was still pregnant, and I had a chance to keep my grandchild alive.

Tears welled up continually, even now as I write this so many years later. I wanted to go see my grandchild. I wanted to die and go see her in Heaven. I couldn't wait another forty, fifty, sixty years to meet her. I wanted nothing else. Nothing on this earth could bring me joy.

I named my grandchild Joy.

The grief! The hidden grief! Losing a child in any way is devastating. But not being able to openly grieve brings its own set of additional emotions and challenges, a heavier cross to bear. No flowers. No cards of condolences. No funeral. No graveside ceremony.

> Losing a child in any way is devastating. But not being able to openly grieve brings its own set of additional emotions and challenges, a heavier cross to bear.

Nothing but a life extinguished as if it had never existed. As if it had no soul. No reason to live. No value. Nothing. Except that it was everything to a grandmother who still openly weeps. *Oh, my darling little grandchild. I see other children hugged by their grandmothers, but I am denied that privilege with you. You were denied the privilege of being loved, of being held, of living your life. What did you do to deserve this?*

Time does heal. But time doesn't heal. Time goes on, and we have to go on. We cope, but life is grey and no longer bright. Talk to anyone who has lost a child and they will tell you this is how it is. Those of us who have lost a grandchild through abortion can't even tell you. We grieve alone.

By God's grace, the Lord sent someone from the pregnancy centre into my path at my point of deepest despair. Someone who understood, who listened to me, who sympathized, offered me desperately needed support, encouragement, and advice, and prayed with me. God met me at the time of my greatest need.

When I was trying to get pregnant, I thought of those who had abortions as selfish, women who had lost their children by choice. I had no pity for them. After what happened with my daughter, I no longer see it that way. So many actually don't have a choice. They are as much victims as those who lose their babies to miscarriage or any other way. Many times, the circumstances surrounding their choice are such that they don't see any other way out. And support for them is often lacking.

My overwhelming feelings were of unending, excruciating grief and the sense that nothing was worthwhile anymore. It could be a beautiful sunny day with lots of good things happening, but everything still felt senseless and meaningless. It was hard to feel good about anything, since I was living life without my grandchild. Many times, I unexpectedly burst into tears. I'd be carrying out some activity and think I was doing okay, then suddenly and without warning I would break down. Random thoughts would occur to me such as, *the tree outside my window is alive, but my grandchild is not.* What irony. It all felt so unfair.

I talked with my doctor who was also the one who sent my daughter for the abortion. She was surprised I had found out, and related to me in seeing it as a baby. She had suggested to my daughter that she tell me about the pregnancy but, understandably considering her position, I don't feel she really pushed for that. Even in my pain, I respected and empathized with the difficult position my doctor had been in. She likely wanted to tell me, but her hands were tied and she couldn't.

Sadly, I don't believe that my daughter was given the option of an informed decision. Our doctor was quick to make a referral, which normally would be a good thing, but not in this case. She told me it would have been too emotional for my daughter to carry her baby, given that it was the result of a rape. That didn't comfort me. It wasn't *her* family she was talking about. It was mine. My flesh and blood. My grandchild.

Why did that innocent baby have to pay the price of her father's sin with her life? Doesn't everyone sin? Maybe not rape, but other sins that don't result in the sacrifice of an innocent human life? My doctor also said adoption isn't as open as I might think. I totally disagree, but even if I hadn't been allowed to see my grandchild after she was placed for adoption, at least she would be alive and would have had the hope of a good life. Abortion didn't offer her that.

I became adamant that abortion is so wrong—full of death and deceit—committing a sin in order to deal with sin. The doctor attempted to assure me that it would be better when our daughter had a child out of love in the future. But how does another grandchild replace the one who died? It doesn't. We love each of the grandchildren that we now have, but none replaces the ones we've lost, and none removes the pain of those losses.

My doctor asked me what I would have done if I had known before our daughter had the abortion. I actually fear that I might have allowed my daughter to terminate the pregnancy, not knowing what I know now. And that is the crux of the problem—that what we don't know about the after-effects of abortion is what leads to so much misery. I now understand that the psychological after-effects are real. I determined to work with my local pregnancy centre to help bring knowledge and information to girls who found themselves pregnant and who were trying to decide what to do.

I will bear the scars of what happened to my daughter and to her unborn child my whole life. As a Christian, I cling to my faith and the support and love I receive from my Lord and Saviour. I long to hold my grandchild, to snuggle her, to tell her that Grandma loves her. One day I will. For now, I rest in the knowledge that she is greatly loved by a God who is infinite love and who will redeem all things.

> *Why, my soul, are you downcast?*
> *Why so disturbed within me?*
> *Put your hope in God,*
> *for I will yet praise him,*
> *my Savior and my God.*
>
> —Psalm 42:5

I held a lot of anger towards my daughter for what she had done in taking my grandchild from me. A few weeks after I found out about the abortion, I was listening to worship music. The lyrics talked about how Jesus comforts the broken-hearted, the discarded. I started to cry again, not for myself this time, but for my daughter. The rage inside me turned into compassion. The Holy Spirit filled me with such love for my daughter that it was overwhelming. I experienced a complete 180-degree turn, a miraculous sovereign healing by God.

It was amazing and beautiful. I had such compassion for my daughter, for what she'd had to go through. I grieved with her and for her. What terrible pain she must have been in! What had she had to endure all alone as she attempted to deal with her grief, her mixed-up emotions, and the terrible situation she found herself in? My heart ached for her. Every one of us has been forgiven so much. How can we not forgive others? I forgave her completely. My heart had been broken, and from then on I knew I needed to be loving and supportive.

A few months later I had the most wonderful dream. My husband and I were so, so happy. A baby was greeting us, reaching out to us, and exuberant to be with us. The child belonged to me completely, although I hadn't given birth to her. She wore a dress that I changed before wrapping her in the yellow blanket I had used to bring our daughter home from the hospital. Her bright blonde hair matched the blanket, and she looked so beautiful. Somehow I knew deep inside that this dream was to let me know that one day I would see my grandchild.

Still, the pain continued. Life is a mix of pain and joy, disaster and hope, trouble and redemption. Our daughter went on to have a second abortion, as apparently many do. And again without our knowledge. How could I be so blind a second time? I grieved for my second grandchild that I would never see in this life. Somehow though, the knowledge that I had lost a second grandchild didn't hit me as hard as it had the first time. Was I becoming callous? Are we all becoming callous to the extinction of little ones as abortion is now so commonplace?

I took this second loss in stride. Or maybe more in denial is a better way to say it. As if it didn't happen. Trying to hide the fact so I didn't feel the pain all over again. But dear grandson, you did exist. Was your life any less precious than any other grandchild? Are you any less loved? Absolutely not.

On some level, did I believe I didn't deserve a grandchild because I hadn't stopped the first one from leaving this earth so prematurely? Was I guilty of either of their deaths in some way? What did I do wrong? Guilt, shame, and self-blame attempted to attach themselves to me. Abortion is not only destructive to the baby, but also to mothers, fathers, families, and the whole of society. The damage manifests in so many ways in the days, months, and years that follow.

I have had help to deal with the pain and loss, and so has my daughter. This help was available through Christian organizations. If abortion wasn't seen as so right—and such an indisputable right—in our society, but truly understood for what it is, would there be more openness to discuss it and more help available? If there was, then there would be less of a chance of people like myself and my daughter walking round with such hidden, suppressed grief. Grief that tends to surfaces at unexpected times and in ways that aren't healthy. If a woman faced with an unplanned pregnancy could be treated, helped, and supported in the same way as someone struggling with an addiction, a mental illness, or any other condition that causes pain, then our society would benefit and people would be healthier.

He will wipe every tear from their eyes. There will be no more death or mourning or crying or pain, for the old order of things has passed away. He who was seated on the throne said, "I am making everything new!" Then he said, "Write this down, for these words are trustworthy and true."

—Revelation 21:4-5

eight

The Days that Change the World

by Jennifer Christie

There are some stories that are easier to get through if they are strongly edited. Take away some of the ugliness, maybe sand out some of the rough patches, and present the whole thing as a tidy package with a nice, sparkly little bow. This is one of those stories. However, I'm not going to do that. I want you to witness firsthand what a tremendous God we serve. How great is His love. How true is His faithfulness.

In my mind, my life is divided into two parts—before I became a statistic and after. Before the rape—"BR"—is a time now unimaginable to me. Now unattainable. Still, what I have discovered about myself, my husband, and my God in the last five years makes the "AR" a far richer existence. In spite of the pain, in spite of the trauma, regardless of fear.

I have a four-year-old son. He's my fifth and by far the youngest child. He giggles in his sleep. He plays with Tupperware in the bathtub. He picks me bouquets of crabgrass and dandelions. He pronounces hospital "hostable." He tells me how much he misses me when I walk to the mailbox without him. And he was conceived in rape. One of those things you wouldn't know just by spending time with him. One of those things that doesn't matter at all.

Not to us, anyway. Not to him.

But I'm getting ahead of myself.

2014. The air was thick. Syrupy. My body felt heavy, but my spirit… empty. There was nothing left. He had taken everything. Several weeks before when the world changed forever.

The day began ordinarily enough as, I suppose, all world-changing days do. I'd been working several hours from home and had spent the week in a hotel. As a sign language interpreter, travel was and is a regular part of the freelancing experience.

Rushing to escape the bitter wind on the last morning of this assignment, I was paying scant attention to my surroundings. A scarf wrapped around my face muffled any sounds of footfalls already quieted by the newly-fallen blanket of snow. The oversized hood of my coat completely obliterated my peripheral vision. So important was fashion back then that I didn't realize I had been followed from the parking lot.

My frozen fingers fumbled clumsily with the key card to my room and, once inside, I turned to close the door. And started. A man stood in the doorway.

Tall. He was so tall. His neck was unnaturally thick. He had the look of someone who spent far too much time at the gym. He appeared young. And clean cut. Remarkable in the fact that nothing was truly remarkable about him at all. Had this been a movie, the ominous music would have already begun by this point. This relatively nondescript kid would take on the form of a comic book villain. His eyes might be aflame, glowing like hot coals, or he could be drooling like a cookie-cutter madman in a made-for-TV drama… but there was none of that. Nothing warned me that I was supposed to feel scared.

And I didn't feel scared.

They say that in moments of danger, your instinct is fight or flight. But it isn't that simple. There is also freeze. You freeze because there is no way this is real. No way this is happening to you. Even if it's only for a breath, a blink, a heartbeat… freezing will cost you. And cost you dearly.

Something *told* me to move. To get away. And I meant to… I mean, I was going to… when he punched me in the head.

It happened so quickly. Dazed, I fought. I fought until I didn't. I fought until I heard before I felt my ribs break. Then my fingers snap. Until I understood that fighting was making it all worse. Might, in fact, get me killed. I tried very hard then to crawl somewhere deep inside of myself. Matthew 10:28 came to mind: *"Do not be afraid of those who kill the body but cannot kill the soul…"* Thoughts whirled through my head. *Whatever is happening to my body, he can't touch my soul. He isn't touching my soul…*

That is what I told myself. That was how I would survive.

I don't know how long I was in that room. It was a place apart from time. Not really though. What felt like it could have been days, weeks, years, even… must have only been hours. Mercifully, I eventually lost consciousness.

My next memory was the sound of a woman screaming, and a rush of cold that felt like a slap. I was lying in an unnatural position, naked save for a piece of a broken bra. It had been a new one. Upside down. Twisted. Bent. I hurt. The aforementioned screamer had covered me with her coat, crooning at me in Spanish. A language I recognized but did not understand. Her words floating into unfamiliar bubbles and pop… pop… popping into fragments of nothingness around my head. She wore the drab brown uniform of the hotel housekeeping staff. Tears streamed down her face. Her name tag read *Lourdes*. We were in the stairwell behind the hotel that led to the dumpsters. I didn't remember how I had gotten there.

In the hospital, I would be treated for the broken bones. A brain bleed that left me epileptic. They removed a broken beer bottle from my colon. The extent of that damage would prove to be so severe that I would need six surgeries over the next few years, including a complete bowel resection. The financial devastation would be enormous. We had no idea. I was given antiretrovirals and a rapid HIV test that came back negative. My chart showed that a morning-after pill was administered. I was in physical and emotional agony. I was terrified. Nothing, nothing made sense.

Nearly six weeks later, I was outwardly pieced together. But I still couldn't wrap my head around what had happened. I didn't know who I was. As a woman. A wife. A daughter. I was so angry. Not necessarily at God… at least, that's what I told myself. Logically, I knew that believers weren't exempt from suffering. In fact, we were all but promised a life of hardship if we followed Christ, but I was stunned at the evil that we as human beings were capable of inflicting on each other. I didn't want to be on the planet anymore. Didn't think I *could* be.

And then it was time to go away again (bringing us to the syrupy air). It seemed like a reasonable decision at the time. I had committed to this work trip, a cruise, months previously. At home, in the early aftermath of the attack? I was coming undone. I wasn't eating or sleeping. I jumped at shadows. I didn't know how to live. My husband, scared for me and unsure of how to process his own anger and grief, thought a change of scenery could only be beneficial for me.

"He's taken enough from us," he reasoned. "We need to get back to our lives." He said that with a painted-on smile. The same smile he'd worn when he told me everything would be okay after I heard him sobbing in the shower and punching the walls. Liar. But what choice did he have? Did *we* have? I left for the cruise.

Day two of a scheduled ten-day excursion, I found myself violently ill. Antibiotics proved futile. As talk of the necessity of a stronger cocktail, perhaps administered intravenously, began, and routine "there's no chance you could be pregnant?" questions formed on the lips of ship medics, I connected to the ground in a very real way for the first time since *that* day.

There *was* a chance. Dear God… something… happened to me. Cartagena, Colombia.

As I slid onto the metal examining table, both soothing and harsh in its coolness, and stared at the ultrasound screen, I would have given anything for a familiar hand to hold. Grainy black and white snow. Meaningless shapes. Then I saw it. Tiny. But unmistakable. A little pea. I knew what it was—I'd seen them before.

I could practically hear the world telling me, "You're pregnant from a brutal rape. You should be angry. Horrified, even! Resentful." But… in that moment? The darkest of my life? I looked at that little pea… and that pea was light. That pea was *hope*. That pea was my baby. *My* baby. And for the first time since the attack, I smiled. I looked at that screen and I smiled at him.

I wouldn't be home for several days still. My husband knew I'd been sick but not why. I couldn't keep this to myself. We had nearly two decades of marriage under our belt and had raised four kids together. We'd gone through a lot, but nothing like this.

I was allowed to use the Captain's quarters. My husband picked up on the first ring. I didn't want to drag it out.

"I'm pregnant."

There was a pause so infinitesimal it was almost imperceptible. Then—

"Okay."

His voice calm. Reassuring. *Infuriating.*

"Okay?! *How* is this okay?? What will we tell the kids?? My parents will freak out! What will your parents say? Everyone knows you had a vasectomy! The stigma… My mind is all *over* the place, how are *you* so calm?!"

I could practically hear him smiling over the phone. This was familiar territory. This we could do. His next words were God-breathed and went straight to my heart. I would never need reassurances as to his feelings again.

"Sweetheart. This child is a *gift*. This is something so beautiful that's come from something so terrible and painful for us. We love babies."

Something fluttered then. Excitement. Joy. "Yes… we love babies."

"We can *do* this, you and me. We can do this. This is going to be awesome."

And we did. And it has been.

Our youngest son, a perfect little boy, all wild dark curls and bright blue eyes, came into the world that fall.

Innocent. Made in the likeness and image of our Creator. We've heard him labeled "evil seed" and "demon spawn" and "rape goblin." Even Christian clergy frequently counsel women to abort under such circumstances. This little boy has brought healing and joy to our entire family. Do I suffer? Yes. The suffering would still be there had I not had a child. I was raped. *That's* the trauma. Through this, my family and I have the opportunity to live out Genesis 50:20, *"You intended to harm me, but God intended it for good…"*

> Do I suffer? Yes. The suffering would still be there had I not had a child. I was raped. *That's* the trauma.

The question of forgiveness comes up rather frequently. Often enough that on one particularly trying day, I wrote the following in response and often share it when I speak:

It's not the day.

It's the days. It's moments.

I am uncomfortable. A vast understatement.

I sip milkshakes through a straw and take tiny bites of pudding because it's all I can manage. I had two back molars pulled yesterday. Teeth that had shattered some months ago during a spate of uncontrollable seizures. Seizures that resulted from the head injury I sustained during the attack. I ignored the pain in my mouth until infection set in, and now here I sit. All chipmunk cheeks and popping ibuprofen that isn't touching my pain. But my toddler here is a tempest (as toddlers are wont to be) and needs a caregiver who isn't on something that comes with a warning to avoid operating heavy machinery.

Being sober minded however has its disadvantages. I can't help but think about the origin of my pain... and I find myself in the position of needing to forgive.

When I mention forgiveness, people assume I mean the rape. That one day. That nightmarish morning into afternoon.

That wouldn't be entirely wrong, but it's more than that.

Not the day.

The *days*.

The moments.

It's the call that will have to be made to our landlord, again, apologizing for not being able to make rent this month because everything we had went to fix my mouth.

It's the blood that won't come out of the bed sheets because even after five surgeries, there is internal damage that remains.

It's the loss of independence when my epilepsy requires a driver, a cook, a babysitter.

I feel angry.

I ask, "Why me??"

I briefly think back to my life before it all.

Not the day.

The days.

The moments.

C.S. Lewis said that everyone thinks forgiveness is a lovely idea until they have something to forgive.

For me, for many, it isn't an idea. It's a daily reality. If you are a follower of Christ, forgiveness is more than a suggestion. It's a command.

And not just for ourselves.

I forgive for my joyful baby. All light and love.

I forgive for my older sons, growing into the good men of tomorrow.

For my daughter who watches me to see how a woman of faith responds when in the valley.

For my devoted husband who needs and deserves a helpmate who is present and whole.

And I forgive for myself. For my Saviour.

So I may become that empty vessel, that tool in His Hands as He molds me into the woman I was born to be.

I'm not looking for pity.

I don't want praise.

I write to anyone else out there who lives in this challenging place of seemingly endless forgiveness. Recognize the blessing in disguise. Spiritual battles, of every sort, keep us on our knees.

The only way battles can be won.

So, today.

Swollen and weary, I forgive.

Seventy times seven and beyond.

I forgive.

The day. The days. The moments.

I forgive.

Psalm 147:3: "*He heals the brokenhearted and binds up their wounds.*"

People become so entrenched in the salacious details of the assault that my life gets represented as a sort of true-crime tale. While that is interesting, it isn't the way we view it. What we prefer to tell is a love story. A love story between a husband and wife. A mother and child. A Heavenly Father and His people.

It's fair to wonder about our future. What we'll tell our youngest. He'll learn about it all eventually. We don't worry too much about that.

See… it never mattered to us. From the moment we knew he existed, he wasn't some "rapist's baby." He was *ours*. And he was *His*. And he was wonderful. We'll tell him that he brought happiness to a home heavy with grief. That he gave his mother back her smile when everyone worried it was gone for good. His tiny heart beat splashes of light into her darkness.

We'll tell him the father he knows? The one who gave him a home and a name? The one who didn't miss an ultrasound scan and who would read him *The Giving Tree* a dozen times a night when he was little and make time to play with him after a fourteen-hour work day—that *was* his father in the truest sense of the word. That man is *proud* to call him his son. He feels honoured to raise him.

We'll let him know that who he is was not determined on one snowy winter morning in a hotel he'll never go to in a state he doesn't live in. Who he is… is just him. The unique fingerprint impressed by God into every soul. He is wrestling with his brothers and dancing with his sister and feeding the dog his vegetables. He is piggyback rides with Daddy and cuddles with Mommy and high-fives from his soccer coach. He is the affection from his grandparents. He is the doting of his godmother and the teasing of his uncle. He is his friends and our friends and neighbours and people all around the world who read about us and have written to tell us what a treasure he is. He is the sum total of his experiences, his perceptions, and all that we pour into his sweet spirit every day. *That's* who he is, and that's who he'll be.

What will we tell him? We'll tell him that we needed him. That we might never have recovered without him.

What will we tell him?

Maybe… we'll just thank him.

We'll thank him.

nine

Secret Sorrow

by Michelle Robertson

Thirty-five years ago, I found myself seventeen, unmarried, and pregnant. A big "whoops." We were too stupid to know that Vaseline and latex don't play well together. I hope they teach that in sex education classes now, as that bit of knowledge would have saved me a lot of heartache. Not everyone comes from God-fearing parents who teach about abstinence, or ultra-liberal parents who educate their kids about appropriate birth control.

I was terrified my parents would find out. I was in my final years of high school and was mortified at the thought of being gossiped about. Anticipating the humiliation I would feel being the "knocked up" girl in school, I decided I did not want to have this baby, so I made a doctor's appointment. My boyfriend at the time had no choice in the matter—I distanced myself from him soon after learning I was pregnant.

My doctor was very clinical and cold while discussing terminating my pregnancy. I don't remember the word *abortion* ever being used. Instead, he used the term "therapeutic D & C." He informed me that the hospital only approved these procedures on a case-by-case basis, and I was to go see another doctor who was on the hospital committee in charge of such matters.

Regarding the upcoming appointment, my regular doctor informed me that, "If you could shed a few tears it would help." I was completely naïve to the political climate with regards to abortion and didn't understand why tears were necessary, but I mustered some up nonetheless. I understand now that they approved the procedure only if the health and/or welfare of the mother appeared to be in jeopardy, hence the crying. Mental health was factored in, so appearing mentally unhinged helped my cause, I suppose.

Apparently it did help, because my case was approved, and shortly after I went in for day surgery. I was put under general anesthetic and my pregnancy was terminated. Not a single person discussed potential future negative impacts of having an abortion. Not a single person tried to talk me out of it or offered alternatives. I only felt judgment and cold stares. No follow-up was advised or offered and life went on again, as planned. Until it didn't.

Within the year I was back with the same young man and pregnant again. I look back now, and I don't recognize that immature and foolish girl. I was still not ready to have a baby, but the thought of going back to my doctor, pregnant again, was too humiliating. I did a bit of research and called an abortion clinic in Toronto. The intake receptionist asked me how far along I was, and I lied and told her longer than I actually thought. For some reason I was afraid they would make me wait, and I was anxious to proceed. She was friendly and set up an appointment for me as casually as if I was seeing a dentist for a toothache.

The day of the scheduled appointment, I drove, alone, to the clinic in Toronto. I parked in a side street parking lot and went in through the back door, as instructed, without really understanding why. After making my way to a seat in a deserted, living-room-type waiting room, I picked up a magazine and waited.

Suddenly people started banging on the front windows and the door opposite where I had come in, yelling things I couldn't decipher. I didn't understand what all the commotion was about. The front door burst open, and a man yelled, "Don't kill your baby!"

Then a woman rushed down a flight of stairs that I hadn't noticed before and urged me up the steps. Several girls sat around a reception area. The room was very quiet; nobody chatted or made small talk. Somehow it didn't occur to me that they were all aborting their babies. I filled out some paperwork, paid a fee, and sat quietly to wait.

Soon I was called into an exam room and instructed to lie on a table with my legs up in stirrups. The doctor peered between my legs, examining me. I don't remember him talking to me, but he said to the nurse, "This one is not as far along as we thought."

Terror gripped me. Would they complete the procedure? They carried on. I was fully awake and could hear various noises and feel weird sensations, but I tried to make my mind be somewhere else. Soon I was sitting in a recovery area of sorts being fed juice and cookies as if I had just given blood. Several other girls sat in the same area. Very little eye contact was made, and no conversation was attempted. I lied and told the nurse someone was picking me up, so I was allowed to leave soon after. Relief filled me as I drove away, trying to smother any guilt or shame that I felt. Things didn't work out with that boyfriend, and I wonder now if that was because he was a reminder of what I had done.

Soon I went off to college, started a new career, and met my future husband, Tim. We started dating and, very early on in the relationship, I found myself pregnant again. My first instinct was to abort. Pathetic, right? Judge me all you want, and you still won't ever come close to how badly I judged myself. I explained to Tim that I was not ready to have a baby, and I planned to schedule an abortion. He didn't like the idea, but didn't exactly know what to do about it.

Off I went to carry on with my day, the decision made. On the way home that evening, without any reasonable explanation, I had a complete turnaround in my attitude. Suddenly I found myself thinking, *we can have this baby; we should have this baby!* I met up with Tim that evening to tell him. Sometime later he let me know that he had been praying that I would change my mind about having an abortion. God answers prayers.

Neither of us was walking with the Lord, obviously. I was far from being a Christian, but Tim read his Bible regularly and had been praying to God to lead him to a woman who believed in God. Tim felt a tug towards a more God-centered life, and he wanted a woman to settle down with. On our first or second date he asked me if I believed in God. Well, believe it or not, I had grown up Catholic, so of course my answer was yes. I guess Tim took that as the answer to his prayers. Clearly his theology wasn't that great yet. Even the devil believes in God, after all.

Within one year of our first date we were married and had a baby boy named Matthew. Matthew is now going on twenty-eight years old and has a wife of his own. It crushes my heart whenever I think of what might not have been if God had not intervened in my life. Then I get to thinking of the two babies that hadn't been given a chance at life because of my choices. Were they boys or girls? What would they have been like?

The pain and shame of what I had done grew as the years went by. Very few people knew the truth. I worked hard at suppressing my dark secret and kept friends at a distance as if they would intrinsically know I was a monster.

After Matthew was born, both Tim and I felt drawn to go to church. I still remember, as if it was yesterday, walking into the sanctuary that first Sunday morning. I strolled in wearing jeans and saw a room full of women in dresses. Some of the little girls' dresses even matched the mothers' dresses. I honestly think I was the only female in pants.

Everyone had Bibles and notebooks in their hands. When the pastor started to preach, they all took notes. I felt very conspicuous and uneasy, but Tim was convinced this was the place we needed to be. Over the next few years, my antagonism towards all things related to church grew. I fought against any spiritual leading. I especially fought my husband's spiritual leading.

Every Sunday I tried to convince him to stay home so we could have a family day. I would argue with him about church-related things and complained that "if I had wanted to marry a pastor, I would have."

By now we had two children, and they were the only things keeping me in this marriage, other than the fact that I was just plain stubborn. Of course, God's grace and mercy was what was holding us together, but I didn't know that yet. At that point I resisted going to church at every turn. Tim took the kids with or without me, and the whole time was quietly patient and praying. That was so alien to me, his behaviour.

Tim kept going to church Sunday after Sunday. Occasionally I would give in and go with him. He continued to be patient and pray. Be sure many people were praying for "that poor man's wife!"

God was answering those prayers and starting to work on my heart, because my antagonism was slowly replaced by openness. Sometime in 1998, I began to attend church more regularly with Tim. God continued to tug at me, and I did my very best to ignore Him. But God is all-powerful, and when He wants something, He gets it!

The reality of what I had done to those two little babies haunted me, and now that I occasionally sat under the preaching of God's Word, the painful reality was magnified a hundredfold.

One particular Sunday, the pastor spoke on repentance and restitution. I can't remember a specific passage; I only remember lying in bed that night completely broken. Weeping for the little babies I had aborted and pleading with God to tell me how I could ever make restitution for the evil sin I had committed. I begged Him to forgive me for what I had done. God's Spirit convicted me that day, revealing to me that I was a wretched sinner, and that I needed His forgiveness and grace to be right with Him.

For years I endured the weight of that conviction without any real sense of the joy that seems to come with conversion for other people. Yes, I was saved when I asked for God's forgiveness. I turned away from a sin-filled life and began to follow the example of Christ in the Bible. But I didn't "feel" saved. My sin was just too great, I believed, and I certainly felt too much shame to talk about it with anybody.

A year or so after I first called on God in faith, I heard a sermon on David's Psalm 51, written in response to his conviction over the sin of adultery he'd committed with Uriah the Hittite's wife. To cover his sin and avoid its consequences, David committed another sin and had Uriah murdered. Psalm 51 is one of repentance, and I completely related to his broken-hearted pleas.

> *Purge me with hyssop, and I shall be clean;*
> *Wash me, and I shall be whiter than snow.*
> *Make me hear joy and gladness,*
> *That the bones You have broken may rejoice.*
> *Hide Your face from my sins,*
> *And blot out all my iniquities.*
> *Create in me a clean heart, Oh God,*
> *And renew a steadfast spirit within me.*
> *Do not cast me away from Your presence,*
> *And do not take your holy spirit from me.*
> —Psalm 51:7-11 NKJV

Upon reading that psalm, I remember thinking that *I* had a broken and contrite heart. In fact, I had it in good measure. From that understanding my faith grew, but I still lacked the assurance of salvation. I still felt God's arm wasn't long enough. I understand now that I was diminishing God's power. I didn't feel worthy of the grace and mercy being offered to me. And I couldn't yet talk about the secret sorrow I carried with me every day.

For many years I sat in church and kept my secret. I felt like an imposter. I felt unworthy and wretched. The pain and anguish got worse as the years went by. I was missing the joy that I saw in so many Christians. God had done a marvelous work in my life when His Spirit performed the miracle of repentance in my heart. Christ's work on the cross bought my pardon with God. No longer would I suffer the penalty I deserved for killing His created beings. I hadn't earned any of that—it was all a gracious gift from God. It was all "amazing grace that saved a wretch like me," but I still wasn't giving God the glory and honour for this incredible work.

Nobody truly understood how incredibly gracious God had been in my life, because I couldn't talk about it. God had forgiven me, but I guess I still hadn't forgiven myself. I continued to drag around the chains of conviction, even though God had released me from the penalty of my sin.

Imagine someone being released from prison but having to keep their hands shackled. That isn't true freedom. I was useless and weak and an ineffective servant for Christ. I felt worthless.

> I was so focused on the pain and shame that I was missing out on the blessings that come with God's forgiveness, grace, and mercy.

I was forgetting about so many promises I had been reading about in the Bible. When God uses us in our weakness, it magnifies His strength. As it says in 2 Corinthians 12:9, *"But he said to me, 'My grace is sufficient for you, for my power is made perfect in weakness'..."*

I was so focused on the pain and shame that I was missing out on the blessings that come with God's forgiveness, grace, and mercy. There is healing when you walk with God. Emotional and spiritual pain can be replaced by joy and hope when God moves in your life.

Psalm 147:3 promises that, *"He heals the brokenhearted and binds up their wounds"* and in John 16:22, Jesus said, *"So with you: Now is your time of grief, but I will see you again and you will rejoice, and no one will take away your joy."* I was not claiming these promises of God. I couldn't stop looking behind me long enough to see what God wanted to do in my life going forward. I was stuck. God doesn't give up though, and His Spirit continued to prompt to me to work through the sorrow I felt, even though all I wanted to do was bury it in the deep recesses of my mind and heart.

A few years ago, God led me to a post-abortion, Bible-based study called *Living in Color: the goal of post-abortive recovery* by Jenny McDermid, held at the local pregnancy resource centre.

The study helps you work through the grief of loss. A grief I wasn't even aware I carried, much less understood. When people die or a woman has a miscarriage, we are urged to work through the grief process. It's healthy and encouraged. The grief of abortion, however, is not readily acknowledged. After all, I had brought this on myself. Did I really have any right to grieve? Through the study, I learned that the profound grief was real. Also, the shame I felt wasn't from God, and through study, prayer, and the encouragement of godly friends, it was slowly taken away. I was reminded, over and over again, how powerful God's forgiveness is. My sin had been blotted out of His mind *"as far as the east is from the west…"* (Psalm 103:12).

The more I talked about the abortions and understood God's healing power, the less I felt restrained by the chains of sin and pain. Only a few short years ago, I couldn't think about what I had done to my babies much less talk about the abortions to others. Now God has healed my broken spirit and is equipping me to share my story. I am now able to speak freely about the awful thing that I agreed to, twice. The abortions caused me many years of guilt, remorse, and anguish. Fear and shame held me back from revealing my true self. I was afraid of judgment if people knew the truth about me. For years I felt as though I was mentally ill because nobody told me I needed to grieve and heal from the trauma of abortion.

People talk about choice and freedom and rights, but few talk about the secret sorrow that women live with after having an abortion. I get angry when I think about the fact that the medical system never warned me about the mental anguish I might feel after terminating my pregnancies.

I recently had gall bladder surgery and the list of possible risks the doctor casually rhymed off was both staggering and terrifying. I was informed of the risks, however, and therefore knew what to be on the lookout for. I had no idea that abortions could cause long-lasting mental trauma, so it was never on my radar. I had no clue that unresolved grief was negatively affecting my interpersonal relationships with family and friends. I had no idea that something I had fully chosen would torment me for years.

Of course, I can't say with certainty that more information would have caused me to choose differently. I am adopted myself, which is a great story. Maybe I would have considered adoption if even one person had explained fetal development to me and not acted as though I was ridding myself of an inconvenient clump of cells.

Maybe, if the doctor had shown me a life-size model of a ten-week-old fetus, I would have realized that this wasn't simply a clump of cells but a tiny, fully-formed baby with hands and feet and a heartbeat. Maybe I would not have destroyed those two little miracles of creation growing inside me.

Maybe my story would have been completely different.

ten

God Heals: A Father's Story

by R. Dyer

Several years ago, I came face to face with something that until then was only a word I had occasionally heard. It was a word that I thought was just an idea that no one actually followed through with. My girlfriend told me she was pregnant and then said, "Don't worry about it; I will take care of it. I'll have an abortion."

What?! Nobody actually does that, do they? Turned out she was serious.

I couldn't believe what I was hearing. The pregnancy I was pretty sure we could deal with, but killing our child made no sense and, as far as I could understand, was not an answer. Abortion went against the principles I believed in living by—you do not ask someone else to pick up your tab, and you surely do not ask someone else to pay for your mistakes. Above all, you do not ask anyone, least of all your innocent, unborn child, to pay with its life for your behaviour. Pretty simple.

We discussed it several times over the next few weeks, but she was adamant that abortion was the solution to our problem. I knew we loved each other, and on that platform, I tried to offer alternative solutions. I suggested we get married, but she argued that pregnancy was not a good reason to marry. Sometime later she said that us getting married would make her the happiest person in the world, but at the time she was not there. I knew she was frightened and that fear was behind her wanting the pregnancy to be over, but I honestly believed that she was jumping from the frying pan into the fire.

I said to her, "I know you—your heart is too big. You can't do this and just walk away." But she was scared. I offered to raise the baby myself, to no avail.

I could not come to terms with killing our baby. The reality was that we had a child. The time had passed to decide if we wanted one or not, we had one. The question now was what did we do with the one we had? Killing it was way beyond my comprehension and something I had never truly believed anyone did. The right thing to do was give this baby the best we had.

In the end, though, I had no say and she set the date. I tried everything I could think of to get her to see that ending this baby's life was not the answer. This was not a case of me against her, it was a case of trying to stop someone I loved from making a bad decision and killing someone else I loved. She saw the situation differently, and our relationship ended.

When I finally grasped that I could not save the baby, I went home, tried to sit on the edge of my bed, missed, and landed on the floor. I spent the next three days there, unable to get up. I was powerless to stop the death of this innocent child, and I was powerless to get up off the floor.

I lived on the second floor of an old house that had a small balcony off the back door. Sometime during those three long days, I dragged myself to the exit and looked out in an effort to determine if I'd suffered a mental breakdown. Everything I saw made sense, so I figured I had not lost my mind. I couldn't figure out why I couldn't leave the apartment, but there I stayed for seventy-two hours. I was shattered—this little child, my child, was about to lose its life because of fear. How could love not prevail?

When I did finally manage to clamber to my feet, the first thing I did was write down a song that came to me. I played it a couple of times and then put it away. Emotionally it was difficult to sing. I had heard nothing about the baby, and I held on to a hope deep inside, like a little flame, that maybe she had changed her mind.

A short time later, while having coffee with a friend, I asked about her, and he told me she'd had the abortion. The little glimmer of hope, the tiny flame, was put out. I left and went to find her. As God would have it, I found her walking down the street. After I'd asked several times, she agreed that we could talk. I simply told her that I didn't want her to go through life thinking I hated her, because I didn't. I told her that I understood, even if I didn't agree with the abortion. I wasn't trying to get back together with her; I truly did not want her to carry with her the thought that I hated her. We said goodbye and I thanked God that we'd had that chance to talk. Now I could move forward.

Those were difficult times for me. Sometimes I felt sad, sometimes bewildered, other times I was in denial, or feeling guilty, and sometimes rage consumed me, yeah rage. I knew I had to face this thing that I never even believed took place. Again and again I asked myself, who would kill their own child? I'd had my eyes forced open to a huge injustice in our world. Not only my child, but countless others were victims to the same plight. I was gripped by a deep, heart-wrenching grief and sorrow that went past cognitive thought. My ex-girlfriend told me later that I had experienced the loss of my innocence.

A good friend of mine often stopped by to see how I was doing. Sometimes he would sit quietly and listen to my broken-heartedness and occasionally my ranting, but he was there and I love him for it. He was a Christian who prayed for me and talked to me about Jesus for years. I had given my life to Jesus a few months before I met my girlfriend. I believe God brought my friend and me together to be fellow sojourners on the journey of trials and tribulations—and jubilations—as Jesus completes the work He began in us.

A couple of weeks after saying goodbye to my ex-girlfriend, I received a call from her. She wanted us to try and get back together. My first instinct and gut feeling was to say no. I still needed to deal with the abortion, to face it and work through it. My second thought was it would be nice to not have to do that alone. Maybe we could do it together. So, we decided to try and build a bridge back to each other.

Over the next few years we saw each other when we could. Occasionally, we would go to church, sometimes shopping, and other times we would simply be together. I held her while she cried and cried over the abortion and said that if she had one thing to do over in her life that would be it.

It was difficult to witness her pain and see how she, too, had been destroyed. The issue we had to face was not only the abortion, but the aftermath of the abortion. The baby was gone, and we were left wounded. It was difficult to look into each other's eyes and realize that we had both put up walls. There was a place inside herself where she would not go, a place in which she hoped to hide from herself something so painful, so difficult that she did not believe she could face it.

And there was a place inside me where the pain, broken-heartedness, anger and rage were housed. I had hoped that we could be there for each other as we took this on, the two of us against our pain, not each other.

We knew of each other's walls. Many times I told her I had to face the abortion and deal with it, that I was not good at running. She countered that I would have to do it alone, because she could not face it. After a few years our relationship ended, not because we did not love each other, for I will always believe that we did. Not because of the abortion, because forgiveness and healing were available to both of us, but you can't heal without facing yourself. I could not run from myself, and she was not ready to face herself. I not only lost my baby, but I lost someone I dearly loved.

Over the next while, I had the opportunity to face and deal with every aspect of the abortion of my child and to deal with it.

One of the first questions I asked God was why He had allowed this to happen. A pastor friend told me that God had no choice, as my ex-girlfriend had a free will; I suggested I should worship her then, because she could over-rule God. In 2 Kings 18, King Sennacherib exercised his free will to attack the towns of Judah. God sent down an angel and wiped out him and his army. God could have stopped the abortion, but He did not. The answer that came to me was that sometimes God chooses not to intervene but allows the natural consequences of our decisions to play out. That was an answer I could live with, although God would have more to say about that later.

I saw a professional secular counselor; he said I should be able to get over the abortion. I never went back. I met a new friend—she had her own story to tell and was very compassionate, kind, and understanding. She was busy speaking, and when I had time, I would drive her around to her engagements. That gave her a little down time between the several talks she would do in a day. One day she asked me to drive her to an engagement and then invited me to speak at it and maybe sing my song.

I thought, okay I can talk about abortion, in a general sense, of course. I had been very focused on the issue and had gathered a lot of information. While we were driving there, she revealed that she wanted me to tell the story of my child. That was something I had never done and was not sure I could.

My friend assured me there would be hardly anyone there, so I shouldn't worry about speaking, it would be fine. When we arrived, the organizer met us in the parking lot and greeted us by saying, "I am so glad you made it; our hall is packed and there are several rows of people standing at the back because we ran out of chairs. This is the most we have ever had in the building."

I prayed and asked God for the courage to stand up in front of all those people and bare my soul, wounds and all. The talk went well. I sang my song to an audience for the first time, and I made it through.

Barely, but I made it. We showed a video about aborted children, and my friend gave a brilliant, honest, and compassionate talk, as usual. We went on to do more talks together, including speaking in schools. I also began to speak on my own. I was not one to get up in front of people, but in God's strength, not mine, all things are possible.

I carried on with my quest to deal with all aspects of losing my child. I faced everything I could from comments people had made, to those directly involved in the abortion. My ex-girlfriend had told me that the abortionist made several comments about me not supporting the abortion. That made things so personal, I believed I needed to deal with what he had said.

I came across 2 Chronicles 7:14: *"If my people, who are called by my name, will humble themselves and pray and seek my face and turn from their wicked ways, then I will hear from heaven, and I will forgive their sin and will heal their land."* The healing of this land and us is not contingent on what the wicked are doing, but is directly related to God's people and their relationship with Him. That would become a main piece of my thoughts and talks and actions—if God's people will be God's people, our land will be restored. I wrote a pamphlet about God's Word, the church, and abortion.

> The healing of this land and us is not contingent on what the wicked are doing, but is directly related to God's people and their relationship with Him.

Jesus continued to speak to me through His Word and His Spirit. When King David's son was taken, he said, "He cannot come to me, but I will go to him." That resonated with me—my child could not come to me, but one day I would go to him or her.

One time Jesus spoke to my spirit three times saying, "There is no such thing as death in the kingdom of God."

Three times I answered, "Yeah, I know."

73

Then He said, "If there is no such thing as death in the kingdom of God, then someone you really love did not die in reality; read the book of Job."

Whoa, whoa, whoa, what? First off, that caused me to redefine what reality is. The world I am in is temporal; the world God is in is eternal. I needed to teach myself how to live in reality. In the last chapter of the Book of Job, God restores Job and gives him back twice as many material possessions as he had lost. But He only gives him back seven sons and three daughters, the same number of children that had been taken from him. Why not double like everything else? Because alive on earth Job had seven sons and three daughters, and alive in the spiritual realm Job had seven sons and three daughters. Job had exactly double, fourteen sons and six daughters, they just happened to be in two different places at that time, but they were all alive. There is no such thing as death in the kingdom of God!

I spoke with a wonderful Christian counselor regarding, among other things, the loss of my child. She was a wonderfully skilled counselor, but upon seeing the rawness of the pain relating to my child, she referred me to someone she defined as having a gift. She told me she would not tell the new counselor anything about me other than that she was making the referral.

I met with this new person. She did not ask why I was there but suggested we pray. When I closed my eyes, the only thing I could see in all different fonts in my mind's eye was a single name. As we prayed, she said to me, "You have a child. He is not with you, but you know his name."

Incredulous, I responded, "Yes, his name is Daniel."

After we prayed, I said, "I always felt the baby was my son, but I thought that, being a man, I would lean that way."

She replied, "I am not a man, and I know it is your son."

Shortly after that amazing encounter, I did a brief tour with an evangelist. One evening I sang my song, and after we were finished a young woman came up to me and said, "When you were singing your song, God's Spirit told me that your son was listening."

I said, "Isn't that interesting, because I did not introduce the song as being for my son, I said my *child*."

She replied, "God said your son was listening." As God often does, He confirmed the truth He had told me: I have a son Daniel, and he is alive. I will see him again, and he heard the song I wrote about losing him. I can't wait to see him and spend eternity together in reality! I renamed the song, "Daniel's Song."

One night I was out to dinner with a friend, and the anger toward the abortionist boiled over in me. When I got home, I dropped to my knees and prayed to Jesus, "I have forgiven this person many times, why does it still bother me?"

Jesus spoke to my spirit and said, "You never told him."

My first thought was that I could live with a little anger once in awhile. Then I said to Jesus, "It's late and I don't want to give him cause to say I was disturbing him. If I feel this way in the morning, I will call him."

My feelings hadn't changed by morning, so I called the man who had performed the abortion, and the receptionist put me right through to him. I said, "As a Christian man, I forgive you for taking the life of my child."

After a long pause, he hung up. The impact on me was so dramatic that I went to speak to a pastor friend of mine. The connection between me and that abortionist was broken; now it was me and God, as Jesus continued to heal and restore me. I never felt any more anger toward that man and have been able to sincerely pray for him.

Sometime later, that abortionist was shot while sitting in his house. He did survive, but as far as I know he was unable to perform abortions again. I was a suspect, but Jesus had supplied me with an iron-clad alibi, even though I didn't know I would need one. He took care of me. I was investigated, but that was the end of it. The shooter was eventually caught. I explained at the time that I was pro-life and that included the abortionist's life.

At the time of the shooting, I had recorded, on my own, several songs with a pro-life theme that I had written and performed on numerous occasions. One of the songs was a plea of the innocent unborn titled, "I Only Want to Live."

Around that same time, I decided I wanted to put up a monument on behalf of Daniel, something to say he had been here, he had existed, but was taken. A Christian organization was willing to put up a plaque, but I did not have the funds and it would have just been one plaque among many.

One day, at the end of a gathering where I had sung a few of my songs, a couple asked for a copy of the lyrics to "I Only Want To Live." They said they spoke in schools and they felt those lyrics would be powerful. Sometime later they called to say a monument to the unborn was being erected and asked if they could submit the lyrics for the monument. I was fine with that.

I didn't hear any more about that for months, and then the couple sent me a picture of the monument with the lyrics engraved on it. I was amazed and thanked Jesus. He had heard my prayer and seen my heart, and in His compassion, He orchestrated something much larger than a plaque. Best of all, I had nothing to do with getting that song on the monument. Jesus had heard my cry and responded. I was and am completely blessed by this monument for Daniel and all the little ones whose lives have been taken. Months later I finally made it to see the monument for myself—what a humbling experience to see your name in stone. God is good.

The words they used from the song, forever etched in that stone, are:

I only want to live, can't you hear my call.
My voice is very weak, because I am so small.

They say that I must go, they say that I must die.
Can't you see my tears, can't you hear my cry.
I only want to live, won't you hear my call.
My voice is very weak, because I am so small.

I still have one heart-wrenching prayer before Jesus our living God, and that is for my child's mother. I pray that she gives her life to Jesus and realizes how forgiven she is. I pray she realizes that He died on the cross so that He could forgive and restore her. If she or any other mother, father, or anyone who has had involvement in an abortion reads this, please realize that God loves you, I love you, Daniel loves you, and we all want to spend eternity with you in reality, in heaven.

eleven

No Spirit of Fear

by Norah Smith[*]

The year was 1977. I was seventeen years old, my period was late, and I was scared to death. I had been dating my boyfriend for two years. We had decided to have sex and there I was. I made an appointment with the doctor and he confirmed my fear—I was pregnant.

When I told my boyfriend, we decided to tell our parents. Somehow I ended up telling both sets of our parents myself.

My dad told me I was not keeping it, and my mom simply cried and didn't say anything. My boyfriend's dad beat him and yelled. His mom accused me of trapping him.

That launched a very difficult time in my life. The doctor told me I could have an abortion—that what was in my womb was just a bunch of cells right now, and that he would refer me. The referral had to go before a board and be voted on. It took weeks, and meanwhile the bump in my belly was growing. My parents didn't want me going out too much, as I was starting to show. No one would speak to me at home because they didn't know what to say. It was very uncomfortable. My feelings for my boyfriend totally turned off. We broke up before the abortion, so he had no say in what happened to our child. I was almost eight weeks along before the board decided I could have the procedure done.

Things moved quickly after that. I was forbidden to see my boyfriend, but that was okay because we had already broken up so he had no idea what was going on. I had no one to talk to because this had to stay quiet. I was so scared and alone.

The night before the abortion I was lying on the bed in my room wishing this had never happened. My mom came in and paced the floor. Clearly, she had no idea what to say. She finally managed to tell me that she didn't condone what I had done, but she still loved me. Then she left. No hugs, no tears. I was terrified and alone.

The morning of the abortion, no one would talk to me or look at me. We were all in the dining room, and Mom and Dad were talking too softly for me to hear. I was deeply ashamed; I felt terrible for causing all this trouble, and so very alone. Someone dropped me off at the hospital, I don't even remember who. The whole experience was like a really bad dream. I was wheeled to the operating room and left in the hallway for what seemed like forever.

No one told me there was another way or that Jesus loved me or that I could be forgiven for what I had done or was about to do. No one hugged me, reassured me, or told me I was going to be okay. The nurses shot hard looks at me. I wanted to apologize for being so disgusting. They wheeled me in and stuck a needle in my hand. When I woke up in recovery I was crying for my baby. A nurse told me to be quiet and lie back down. Still groggy from the anaesthetic, I got dressed and went out front to wait for my ride. I wanted to die. It was like my body went into mourning for my baby. I was very sore and scared. And I felt so violated.

When I got home, I went straight to bed because I felt awful. My dad told me to get up and vacuum the house, even though they had told me at the hospital not to exert myself, and the bleeding was really heavy. He looked at me with such disgust. All I wanted to do was make him love me and forgive me, but as the days passed, things grew worse between us.

The only time I was permitted to leave the house was to go to school. The whole year was filled with self-loathing. I hated myself, and I felt as though everyone around me hated me too. A thought began to grow—that if my dad and others thought I was a tramp, I might as well be one.

One night, when my dad was working the afternoon shift, I pulled on my tightest jeans, applied heavy make-up, and headed uptown. Two men in a car pulled over and asked if I needed a ride. I said yes. The desire to punish myself was so overwhelming that I was willing to sink deeper into the abyss. I climbed into the car. The men asked me a lot of questions, one of which was whether I looking for a good time. Again, I said yes, and they drove to a back road.

I don't know why, but before anything could happen, the driver turned the car around and drove me back to the spot where he had picked me up. I was deeply hurt and rejected, but I shrugged it off and got out of the car. Every attempt I made to degrade myself ended the same way—it would go so far and then it stopped. I didn't know it then, but that was God saving me from myself.

Still, I wanted to hurt myself really badly. Before the abortion, I was on the honour role at school, and was obedient and respectful. I was a virgin. *Look where that got me.* I might as well be who they thought I was.

However, gradually my feelings for my boyfriend came back. He had been my best friend and we had done everything together. I loved him very much. I sneaked around and called him all the time, and when I turned eighteen, he bought me an engagement ring. I showed my dad, thinking he would be happy for me, but instead he asked me to leave the house. As soon as I graduated, I moved in with my boyfriend. We were married ten months later in front of a justice of the peace at the courthouse.

We have two lovely children whom we adore, and two wonderful grandchildren, but the abortion continued to be a constant source of pain and shame and hurt throughout our marriage. For years I was on antidepressants. My husband promised we could renew our wedding vows at our 10-year anniversary. He was saved, and he and the kids attended a Pentecostal church. I didn't go with my family, because I thought God would "get me" if I set foot in a church.

My husband asked his pastor if we could renew our vows and he said no because I was not a Christian. I was angry and decided to go to church the following Sunday to speak with this pastor. I sat in the pew with my son and listened to the message. For the first time, I heard that Jesus loved me and that I could be forgiven for my sins. Tears streamed down my face and I didn't know why.

The pastor asked if anyone wanted to pray the sinner's prayer. I raised my hand and he asked me to come forward. My son came with me and we gave our hearts to the Lord together. I had never experienced anything like it. Instantly the love of God washed over me like a huge wave, and I knew without a doubt that I had been washed clean. I had been forgiven and set free of all the shame, anxiety, depression, and fear. I cried for three days. I told anyone who would listen about Jesus and His forgiveness and love. Everyone at work saw the difference in me.

> When I gave my heart to Jesus and started to read the Bible, the first thing God showed me was what *He* thought of me and who I was in Him.

I read the Bible, attended every church service, and prayed every moment of the day. Soon I was off all medication, and I wrote a thank you card to my psychiatrist to tell him about my salvation and to let him know that I wouldn't need his services anymore.

When I gave my heart to Jesus and started to read the Bible, the first thing God showed me was what *He* thought of me and who I was in Him. He revealed to me that He had redeemed me and set me apart for His will. That I was chosen by him, that I am the righteousness of God in Christ Jesus. I am loved, set free, and washed clean by the blood of the Lamb!

The joy of the Lord filled me. It took time, but slowly I started to see myself as God sees me.

One day, someone from the pregnancy centre spoke at our church. Afterwards, she left brochures and I picked one up on post-abortion trauma counseling. I prayed about it and asked God who I could give it to. His answer was me. He wanted to take me through the healing of my abortion.

I was so scared because I had never told anyone but my boyfriend and our parents about the abortion. It took a while to work up the nerve, but I finally made the appointment and prayed that, whoever the counselor was, she would be a strong, godly woman. God's presence could be felt so strongly throughout the whole session. Lisa was my counsellor; she was an RN, and God worked powerfully through her. She gave me scripture verses on fear. When I asked her why, she told me we have an enemy and he wants me to remain a captive of fear. But God desires to set me free. To truly understand what that means, I needed to be able to speak the Word and get it in my Spirit.

Lisa assured me that memorizing scripture on fear was very important, so I memorized John 14:27, "*Peace I leave with you; my peace I give you. I do not give to you as the world gives. Do not let your hearts be troubled and do not be afraid.*" 1 John 4:18 told me that, "*There is no fear in love. But perfect love drives out fear …*" and 2 Tim. 1:7 revealed to me that "*… the Spirit God gave us does not make us timid, but gives us power, love and self-discipline.*" Those were three verses that I never forgot.

During counselling, Lisa instructed me to imagine that everyone who was involved in the abortion sat in a chair in front of me, one at a time. As I did, I was able to tell them how they had hurt me. Later, imagining them on that same chair, I had to forgive each of them. I even got to ask Ruth Anne, the name I had given my unborn baby, to forgive me too. Lisa said she was with Jesus, so she would for sure forgive me, but it was so hard to ask her. Still, it was incredibly powerful.

Lisa gave me a ceramic baby to represent her, and I was able to write an obituary and bury her, symbolically. After all those years, I was given the opportunity to grieve my child and to go through all of the stages.

The anger I had was so big that I would shout and scream and cry. I spent so much time on my face before God. Nothing was left out, and by the time the course was finished, the healing was complete. When I told someone about my abortion for the first time, I wailed like a wounded animal. Thank God she was a good friend, because I sobbed for hours.

My husband even came to counselling with me once. Lisa was so surprised. She started toward us and then made a beeline for the office. A group of women were in there praying for our session, and she told them my husband was here. They were happy he had come to support me. When she told them, "He is the father!" they stayed in there and prayed for us for twenty minutes.

I'll never forget when Lisa wanted me to walk in the right-to-life march. I was very apprehensive and nervous that someone there would know I'd had an abortion. Still, I went and I brought the kids too. They didn't know about my past but came with me most places. It was a powerful experience. God showed me that I was not the same person I used to be. By His grace, it was as though the past had never happened.

Sadly, some of the marchers looked down on people who'd had abortions, but I walked in mercy and sadness for the women who are lost and dying and don't know there is another way. Who have never been told that there is a Father who doesn't think they are dirty and disgusting. An all-loving, all-caring Father who longs to show them real love. The love He showed me.

God called me to go back to school for medical secretary and computer programming certificates. I graduated with honours and was able to attend graduation this time with both my husband and a friend there to celebrate with me.

After I graduated, I got a job in a GP's office. It was wonderful until the day a girl came in for a referral for an abortion. I hung my head and cried and told the doctor that I couldn't be a part of the chain that ended the pregnancy. I started to gather my things, because I was sure I would be fired. He was angry and said it was part of my job, but his wife did not want to lose me. She spoke with him and he was okay with it.

I asked him if I could tell the girl that there were other options and help out there for her. He agreed, so I told her that Jesus loved her, and that if she went through with it, she would regret it. She understood that I knew what I was talking about. I gave her the phone number for the pregnancy centre, and she ended up keeping her baby! When she brought her baby to the office to show me, I cried, partly because no one had told me what I had told her, but mostly because I was so happy for her and her baby.

I've gone on to work in an ob/gyn office and have been able to speak to many women. A friend of mine—who also works for the ob/gyn—and I prayed constantly that the abortions would stop. Now there are no abortions done in the hospital I work at—praise God!

I led my mom to the Lord when I asked her to forgive me for the abortion. She saw how forgiven and loved I was because of the salvation I received through Christ Jesus. The guilt and shame she had felt since I'd ended my pregnancy was enormous. Now our relationship had been healed and was better than ever. My dad and I also reconciled. He went in for an operation and had a reaction to the anaesthetic. His brain swelled and he presented as though he had dementia. The medical staff talked about putting him in a nursing home, and he was only fifty-nine years old. I took a week off from work to be with him and to spend the time praying for his healing around the clock. I wrote scripture verses on slips of paper and left them everywhere in his hospital room.

One day he got up to go to the washroom, and when he came back, I noticed his feet were dirty. I filled a basin with water and set his feet in it. He hesitated for a moment then he let me wash his feet. His healing was almost immediate! We were so in awe of the power of God. Dad and I talked when he got home, and he told me he had given his heart to the Lord years ago when he was just a young boy, but after what happened in the hospital, he rededicated his life to God. My mom and dad have since gone on to glory, and I know Ruthy is sitting on their laps loving them and they are loving her.

My husband and I have been married thirty-nine years and been together for forty-four years, which is a miracle because statistically it never should have worked... but God! We hardly ever really talk about the abortion, mainly because of the feelings that come back when we do. We have not told our children, as of writing this story, but there will be another chapter in which God has healed our relationship completely, and my children will know they have a little brother or sister in Heaven that we will meet one day.

twelve

Fearfully and Wonderfully Made[2]

by Corrie

I adore a good love story. Especially one where an individual over-comes impossible odds and renews our faith in humanity. Perhaps I feel that way because I was part of an impossible love story from the moment I was conceived.

From the day my parents met and started dating, they dreamed of having a family. My mother was training to be a registered nurse and had all the compassion and gentleness an ideal mother should possess. She taught Sunday school at her local church and the kids adored her. She was known for her fun, interactive lessons, for bring-ing in cupcakes when there was a birthday, and for hosting pizza par-ties. No wonder she was the most beloved teacher.

In those days, my parents often talked of having a large family. They joked about raising a "small sports team" and dreamed of being there for each child as he or she grew up. However, after marriage this dream was dashed. They were informed they couldn't have chil-dren. My mother was heartbroken, and my father grieved that the one thing she so desperately wanted in life was being denied her.

Undaunted, my mother suggested that they adopt and give a loving home to a child who really needed one. They were approved and eager to adopt a little boy, but at the last moment the teen moth-er changed her mind and pulled him from adoption. My parents

---

2 A shorter version of this story was originally printed in the Guelph and Area Right for Life newsletter.

were distraught. The nursery was all set up, ready and waiting for their little boy. Still, my mother, encouraged by the hope that there was a child out there in need of a family, applied for adoption again.

During their second application, they were denied adoption. The reason: my mother was deemed an "unfit mother" because of her lupus. Lupus is an autoimmune disease that comes in varying degrees of severity and can affect any organ in the body. However, many women have healthy, thriving lives with families despite having the disease. Despite the fact that she lived a normal life, and was otherwise young and healthy, Adoption Canada determined that her disease disqualified her. My father was livid. My mother was devastated. All she wanted was to be a mother to a child.

After the pain of trying to adopt, my mother still held on to her hope and suggested sponsoring impoverished children overseas. After 11 years of marriage and helping multiple children across the globe, my mom discovered the impossible: she was pregnant. With her history of lupus and kidney disease, pregnancy was risky, but she wanted a child more than anything, so she was willing to take a chance. Then her specialist dropped a bomb. He insisted she have an abortion, as her pregnancy was deemed life threatening. Her kidneys were only functioning at 60 percent, and in his opinion a "therapeutic abortion" was necessary.

My mom was crushed. She had wanted a child all her life. She had dreamed and prayed to be a mother, and the idea of having an abortion, choosing to kill this miracle baby, was unfathomable to her. She worried about what to do and felt pressured by her doctor. My mother's journal entry at this time showed a concerned and upset woman trying to make the right decision without a lot of support. She felt isolated and alone in her choice and pressured to follow through with the doctor's demands for a therapeutic abortion. I can only imagine the stress and fear she must have felt.

When my mom came home after being told she needed an abortion, she turned to her main source of comfort and guidance, her Bible. She prayed and came across Psalms 139:13-16.

For you created my inmost being;
you knit me together in my mother's womb.
I praise you because I am fearfully and wonderfully made;
your works are wonderful,
I know that full well.
My frame was not hidden from you
when I was made in the secret place,
when I was woven together in the depths of the earth.
Your eyes saw my unformed body;
all the days ordained for me were written in your book
before one of them came to be.

Encouraged by these words from David in the Psalms, my mother decided against an abortion, despite the risk to herself. She had carefully considered all possible outcomes of her decision: her and the baby dying, her dying and the baby surviving, or the hopeful outcome of mother and child both surviving. She couldn't take the life of her child out of fear for her own life. She wouldn't take her child's life. If there was a risk, we would face it together. But she would not sacrifice her child to guarantee her own survival. Despite her convictions, it was not an easy decision to make, and she was scared.

When she told her doctor, he claimed she was crazy and suicidal. He refused to treat her and dumped her as a patient, abandoning her without prenatal care. Instead of supporting her, the doctor who was supposed to walk with my mom through her pregnancy turned against her and abandoned her in her hour of need.

Thankfully, her rheumatologist offered to step in until another specialist could be found. He noted that he didn't specialize in babies, but he would help until a medical team was in place.

The next few months consisted of medical appointments with lupus specialists, rheumatologists, nephrologists, and neonatal specialists as my parents prepared for a challenging pregnancy. I was so small that my mother didn't even look pregnant. When she told people she was expecting, they didn't believe her. While I didn't add much in terms of weight, I did put great strain on her kidneys that were already functioning at only sixty percent. Due to this risk, my mother was admitted to hospital for close care and observation at six months.

My mother went into kidney failure at thirty weeks gestation (healthy babies go to forty weeks). My father had just left the hospital where he had played Trivial Pursuit, a board game, with my mother who was not feeling well. As he walked in the door to their home, the phone was ringing. When he picked up, the hospital told him that my mother was going into kidney failure. They needed to take the baby by emergency caesarean, but no incubators were available. Thus, my mom was being moved to St. Boniface Hospital in Winnipeg where there were available incubators.

My dad jumped into the car and rushed to St. Boniface. When he arrived, the ambulance was unloading my mother on the stretcher. As he ran alongside her, down the hospital corridors, the surgeon called out, "Do you want me to save your wife or your child?" The question was unthinkable for my poor father. Both. He wanted both to survive.

I was born by emergency caesarean two months and two weeks early and weighed in at 2.2 pounds. My expected due date was May 5th but I arrived Feb 27th. I was rushed to the neonatal care unit and put on a respirator in an incubator.

At the time of my birth, the foramen ovale, a small opening in the heart that is supposed to close before the baby is born, was still open. I stayed in the intensive care nursery for 100 days. My mother was in ICU for three days and remained in the hospital for one month. I was so tiny that my dad's wedding ring went all the way up to my shoulder, and I fit in the palm of his hand. He later joked that I could have fit in his pocket. Preemie clothing and diapers were too large for me, so ladies from our local church sewed doll clothes for me to wear when I was released from the hospital. I couldn't even cry as my lungs weren't developed, so I spent many weeks red-faced and silently screaming when blood work was done. When I finally did cry, the nurses excitedly called my dad over to the incubator to hear me. He says that I sounded like a kitten meowing.

Since I was delivered so early, my parents weren't prepared for my arrival. The nursery wasn't finished, items still needed to be purchased, and they didn't have a name. I spent a number of weeks listed as "Last name, Baby girl" on the hospital files, the incubator tag, and on my anklet ID. The nurses kept pestering my father to pick a name, as they didn't want to keep calling me by my last name. Eventually, my parents settled on Corrie.

My father's daily schedule consisted of getting up for work, swinging by the pizza place, driving to the hospital to see my mother, and giving a pizza to the nurses on shift (they loved it when he brought pizza). Then he would go down a few floors to visit me in the neonatal ICU.

At neonatal he had to gown up head to toe like a surgeon. He would pull on a blue gown, bootie shoe covers, a hair net, and a face mask before scrubbing his hands, fingertips to elbows with the pink antibacterial soap. After rinsing his hands, he was instructed to hold them upright so the unclean water didn't drip back down, re-infecting his clean hands.

Sometimes he had to wear gloves. Only after suiting up and washing thoroughly was he allowed to enter the nursery and visit me where I usually lay froggie-style (spread out on my stomach). I was hooked up to a number of devices including a heart rate monitor, bladder catheter, and an IV. The IV was attached at my scalp and covered with half a plastic medicine cup, taped to my head to prevent the needle from being knocked or pulled out.

If it was a good day, he could hold me. The bottles provided for feeding were preemie size with smaller nipples to help with drinking. Despite the reduced size, I was still too tiny a preemie to drink on my own. The nurses would intubate me to feed me as I couldn't drink. Only after 100 days in NICU, when I was moved to a regular nursery, would I finally take my first few sips, only to fall asleep in sheer exhaustion from the effort.

Then the nurses would intubate me and give me the rest of my meal. Oftentimes they left cute notes for my parents with updates such as "Corrie set world record. Drank 3 ccs today." Formula was measured in ccs, or cubic centimetres, the measurement commonly found on syringes. I drank, at most, the equivalent of half a tsp before passing out. After visiting me and saying goodnight to Mom, Dad would head home, go to bed, and get up the next morning to do it all over again. I don't know how he managed it. He jokes that I gave him his white hair.

While I was in the neonatal unit, my mother was recovering in the ICU. It was a slow recovery, and when she was finally well enough to come see me, she didn't want to. She was terrified that if she saw me, she would fall in love with me, and having loved me she might lose me.

My father wouldn't accept that excuse. One day he put her in a wheelchair and pushed her down to the neonatal unit. Even as a nurse and medical professional, she was too scared to touch me. When my dad asked why, she said she didn't want to break me as

I was so fragile and small. Dad reassured her I would be fine and placed me on her chest.

From that day forward, we spent many special moments in the NICU bonding as mother and daughter. However, it wasn't until I received my first parcel in the mail, a baby gift from my Aunt Gail addressed to *Corrie*, that my mother realized I was actually here. I was real, and I was a unique person in my own right who wasn't going away. Perhaps she had been in shock or in fear of losing me, but the parcel addressed with my name changed her focus from worry to the realization that I was alive and not going to leave her.

My birth hospital, St. Boniface Hospital, is a Catholic hospital that still exists in Winnipeg, Manitoba. They gave my family excellent care and saved both our lives. One of the best aspects of the hospital was a chapel on the second floor. My father used to visit it and pray for my mother and me. While there, he met a nun who offered to pray for our family and visited me daily at my incubator. At that time, I was not yet named, so she would address me as her little *baba*.

When I grew up to be a toddler, I became quite attached to a pink bunny that I dutifully named *Baba*. It surprised my mother as we had never used that word before and we only spoke English in the home. In some languages, the word *baba* translates to baby, so perhaps the nun who visited me called me her little baby. In any case, I'm thankful that she prayed over my incubator daily and visited my family, offering support and encouragement. She was a bright light of hope during a time of fear and worry.

Our home church also offered faithful support, praying for my mother throughout her pregnancy, and for us both after I was born. They sewed clothing for me, brought meals, and generally offered to help in any way possible.

Thanks to the care at St. Boniface Hospital, fortified by prayers from the sisters there and from my home church, my mother and I pulled through. I'm now in my thirties, healthy and happy. I have a

PhD and teach at a university. I also publish novels, children's books, and academic articles. Every day I'm thankful my mother courageously stood up for me, said no to an abortion, and risked everything to bring me into the world. I'm here because of her love and sacrifice.

I'm also so thankful for the loving support and strength that my father offered during this time. He consistently cared for my mother and me, checking in on us daily at the hospital, and encouraged my mother when she was fearful of losing me. Nothing was guaranteed and my progress was touch and go at times, but my father never lost faith that things would work out. He was the first person to bring my mother and me together after my birth. He encouraged her to move past her fear and to reach out to me, no matter how tiny and frail I was. Once my mother took that step, she was forever bonded with me. We were like sisters, best friends, yet mother and daughter all rolled into one. We used to finish each other's sentences and often had the same songs stuck in our heads at the same time. Our bonding and love were immeasurable.

> The strength that she needed to make the decision for life came not from herself but from her trust and faith in God.

Every day I wake up, open my eyes, and have a new day before me because of my mother's one choice—her decision to fight for me, to bring me into the world—and my father's strength of character in supporting her and our family on that journey.

The strength that she needed to make the decision for life came not from herself but from her trust and faith in God. She turned to Scripture in her time of need, she listened to the promptings of the Spirit of God, and she trusted that God would provide her with the strength to follow through. She trusted that He would be there with her every step of the way no matter what happened, because she was obedient to His voice. Despite fear, despite worry, despite people telling her she was wrong, despite medical experts pressuring her to have an abortion, she listened to the Word of God, and I am alive today because of her obedience.

Had my mother listened to her doctor who told her she needed to have a therapeutic abortion or she would die, I would have been aborted and gone from this world. Her doctor was wrong. My mother didn't die. She survived. We both survived. It was not an easy journey and it was not without its moments of fear. But as Franklin D. Roosevelt famously said, "Courage is not the absence of fear, but rather the assessment that something else is more important than fear."

For my mother, the life of another individual human being, her child, was more important than fear, more important than her own security. I will forever be thankful for the choice she made that day after reading David's words, *"For you created my inmost being; you knit me together in my mother's womb. I praise you because I am fearfully and wonderfully made…"*

I'm alive because one woman—my mother—chose life. And I am forever thankful for those who came alongside us on the journey. Above all, I'm thankful for the faithfulness of God and His blessing and gift of life. I am thrilled to enjoy life every day thanks to one woman's act of obedience in listening to a still small voice.

thirteen

A Father's Perspective on Corrie's Story

by Ron

To have my wife come home and tell me "my doctor wants me to have an abortion" was like having a knife thrust through my heart.

My wife and I were expecting our first child and very early in her first trimester, Nancy was told by her doctor that he wanted her to have an abortion. The reason for this was her existing medical condition—he was concerned about her health and the health of the child.

After many long discussions and time in prayer, she decided that having an abortion was completely wrong. Her doctor was very upset with her decision and informed her that he would no longer look after her and she should find another doctor. This was a devastating blow to her as she was already living with a chronic disease called lupus. To now be told she had to find another physician was overwhelming.

Our family had never really understood or talked about the word *abortion*. Until it impacted our lives, it seemed to be one of those unused words that only applied to other people. I now understand the emotional challenges and the difficulty that women go through when they are faced with the decision to continue with their pregnancy or abort their child. In my mind, abortion was the elimination of a life—that is what I would call murder. However, in other people's minds, it is a convenient way of avoiding something that they did not want or had not planned for. I believe that it is so wrong. I also now know that there is support and assistance for anyone dealing with an unwanted pregnancy.

Over the next six months, our days were filled with questions and many challenges as we struggled with the ongoing pressures of not conforming to the "abortion is a woman's right" band wagon and living the emotional ups and downs of the decision to go through with a high-risk pregnancy.

We were concerned about both my wife and our baby's health and future. This only increased when we found out that Corrie was coming early. Although she was ten weeks premature and very tiny, we believed that God had a purpose for her life. My wife and I both battled in prayer and with our emotions to walk down this difficult path. I can say that as a father the emotional drain on me—the pain I saw in my wife each morning as she dealt with her health and questioned if everything would be okay—was incredible. I guess what I would say is that sometimes making the right decision is very, very difficult. Especially when the life of not only your child, but also your wife, hangs in the balance.

I now look back and realize how incredibly strong and courageous she was to have not given in to pressure and to have remained true to her beliefs. To say that our story is one of success would be an understatement. God was faithful, and although Corrie lived in the intensive care unit for the first hundred days of her life, today she is a beautiful young woman. Corrie has completed her PhD and is now teaching at a university.

When her mother and I look back on the decision we made, a decision that was unspeakably difficult and, at times, put us under severe pressure, we know we did the right thing. I would never, ever want to discount or underestimate the amount of pressure, stress, and fear that comes when you're faced with a decision like this one. However, I do know that a life begins at conception, and that God has created each of us for a very unique and special reason.

If faced with that decision again, I know that we would not change anything. I am so glad that Nancy was strong in her faith and believed that saying no to abortion was the right thing to do. Every day we thank God for our little girl.

fourteen

The Promises Before Me

by Aly Ostrowski

W hen I was sixteen, I was dropped off by my boyfriend's social worker at an abortion clinic not far from home. I remember stepping out of the black Jeep and climbing the concrete steps alone and paralyzed with fear. As soon as I walked through the door, I was told to change into a gown and take a seat in the waiting room. After several agonizing minutes, a nurse called my name and I entered into a dark room with an illuminated surgical bed in the centre where I was instructed to lie down.

I was terrified.

After my legs were placed in stirrups, the male doctor appeared and both he and the nurse studied the ultrasound to make sure they had the right location of my baby. I never got a chance to witness this image first hand. With what sounded to me like a strange exuberance, the nurse asked if I was okay, and then proceeded to explain what would happen and how I could expect to feel.

The next thing I remember is lying on my boyfriend's bed in his cold, drafty room. I was gripped by painful cramps, a sense of heavy nausea, confusion from the drugs, and a feeling of hollow barrenness that would follow me well into my thirties.

This was not the first incidence of trauma in my life. I was sexually assaulted and raped in my early teens, which rendered me unable to discern healthy relationships, understand boundaries, or even think in a rational, cohesive manner. My mind was fragmented.

Although I somehow managed to get good grades in high school, I skipped class regularly to spend time with my dropout boyfriend who was emotionally abusive. We smoked pot and indulged in other recreational drugs.

Both of us battled mental health issues. For me, it was a chronic depression that left me feeling worthless and suicidal. We regularly engaged in sex, always without protection because that's what he preferred, and I didn't have the confidence to say otherwise. We were sixteen, two young misfits, reckless and lost with no concern for the consequences of our decisions. In the midst of this relationship, I found myself pregnant.

The moment I found out I had conceived was miraculous. I was on a family vacation and I woke up in the early morning, stood near the dark hotel curtains, and felt a kernel of life pulsating from my womb. The sensation was amazing. Before I could begin to imagine the potential this spark was harnessing, panic struck and fear sank in. For a young, conservative Catholic girl with an affluent family and impressive academic streak, this pregnancy was an inconvenient and distressing reality. If I were to keep the child, my image at school would be destroyed, my family and friends would scoff, and strangers would judge me for my careless behaviour. In that moment, my pride collided with my fear and the decision was made. I would have an abortion.

> While the enemy was feeding me lies of doubt and insecurity, Jesus was right next to me, speaking hope and promise.

Only after I formed a relationship with Christ did He reveal to me where He was at that time. While the enemy was feeding me lies of doubt and insecurity, Jesus was right next to me, speaking hope and promise. Whatever transpired, He would provide, comfort, and equip. He was assuring me that without fail I would raise a beautiful daughter, and our story would bring glory to His name.

Instead, I panicked and decided to bury the humiliation of my pregnancy. I couldn't imagine carrying the weight of this reality in the midst of my circumstances. I wish that I had only tasted and trusted the faithfulness and all-consuming love of Jesus, which would have given me the strength to conquer what I deemed utterly impossible.

Instead, I got out of that Jeep, walked up those stairs, and went into the clinic.

Throughout the rest of high school and well into university, I continued to hide the secret of my abortion. I became increasingly numb and mentally disturbed. I drank and smoked pot regularly and started to self harm through cutting. I was depressed and under a lot of strain as I faced the stresses of a heavy course load in addition to the fault lines of trauma buried deep within.

I was in and out of therapy, but every time the abortion issue was uncovered, I would tense up, curl inward, and stare off into space, completely unaware of external prompts to reengage. Eventually, something would register, and I would practice my coping routines by rapidly shifting my gaze to different colours, shapes, and textures around the room while physically stretching out my body and breathing in regular, deep rhythms.

In time, therapists chose to avoid this topic altogether because of the intensity of my response. They were unable to loosen the grip of this trauma and opted to address other outstanding problems I was facing. I was discouraged and overwhelmed. It seemed that I couldn't get the help I needed, even from trained psychologists. At that time, I had no access to a resource that could address the root of my emotional pain and bring me to freedom.

Upon completing my undergraduate degree, I fell into my first psychotic episode. I became a missing person and lived in the woods outside of Hamilton for a month. I went completely insane. I was filled with religious grandiosity and experienced profoundly tormenting thoughts that convinced me to run across a six-lane highway in the peak of the day and put cigarettes out on my legs.

As I stumbled through the landscape, I was unable to care for myself, leaving me starving, dehydrated, physically scarred, and medically unstable when I incurred a blood infection after my wounds were exposed to sewage and soil. Eventually, I had a violent confrontation with police and was hospitalized for months. After receiving a formal diagnosis of Bipolar I, I experienced three more psychotic episodes in the next five years, each with their own risks and repercussions.

Even at the leading mental health care institutions, doctors couldn't find out why my illness was so severe, especially since they could find no genetic trace that could be linked to such drastic symptoms. Interestingly, none of them inquired into my past trauma, including the abortion I had experienced when I was younger. That truth stayed dormant for a few more years.

In 2012, my dad, a born-again believer, invited me to a church to listen to a prominent speaker. During that meeting on September 21st, I surrendered my life to the Lord. That was the beginning of the wildest, most profound healing journey I could ever imagine. I had no idea the love that awaited me!

My new community of friends prophesied a great calling on my life and filled me with hope and great anticipation for the promises that lay before me. However, at my core, I was still mired in shame, grief, and profound guilt. How could God ever forgive such a sin? I felt as though I had been branded with a scarlet letter that marked my disqualification for full access to Heaven's blessings and, most importantly, His approval.

In 2015, I had a chance to experience the ministry of Bruce and Evelyn Miles through Restoring the Foundations. For the first time, counsellors attributed the psychotic episodes I had to the curse of the abortion. That was a profound revelation. Over the course of a week, I repented of my sin, was delivered, and experienced a powerful transformation—I could hear clearly from the Holy Spirit, I was awakened to the Father's love for me, and I recognized my identity as a victorious overcomer, a daughter and child of God.

Upon graduating from a Master's program, I started teaching first grade and was astonished to report complete mental stability for three consecutive years, which I could only partially attribute to the medication I was on. Finally, after growing in my faith and believing for deep inner healing, my prayers were answered. I had been seeing a Christian therapist, and she recommended I look into the Post-Abortion Recovery (PAR) Program through the Atwell Centre in Hamilton, Ontario. I was a bit apprehensive about revisiting my abortion, but understood that Jesus died so that my soul could be *fully* free and that He would give me the courage and grace to traverse this journey.

I reached out to family and friends and boldly declared that I was entering into a vulnerable time of reflection and healing. Although I would have the Holy Spirit to guide and comfort me, I would also be relying on the prayers and ongoing support of the women I held most dear.

Within days of contacting the centre, I participated in a sensitive intake process. By the following Tuesday, the lead therapist had established weekly sessions for me to participate in. Every morning I was eager to wake up and do my homework as set out in the activity book. Those chapters took me through identifying my "abortion wound" and reflecting on the complex emotions surrounding my decision including the relief, denial, and avoidance of this event. The book laid the groundwork for a deeper exploration of my pain by identifying Godly conviction and responsibility as a contrast to the crippling shame, fear, anxiety, and depression I had experienced for seventeen years.

During this time, the Holy Spirit revealed critical Scriptures that I clung to in order to anchor my hope and identify with the truth set before me in Christ. For example, Isaiah 44:22 says, *"I have swept away your offences like a cloud, your sins like the morning mist. Return to me, for I have redeemed you."* Through the cross, Jesus had washed away the stain of the abortion. God had so completely forgiven me for the abortion that I didn't even have a right to bring it up anymore. The issue had been resolved—paid for in full. From the moment I gave my life to Him, God saw me as a spotless bride, a woman who had been redeemed and made whole.

The final vindication came from Isaiah 61:7, where it is written, *"Instead of your shame you will receive a double portion, and instead of disgrace you will rejoice in your inheritance. And so you will inherit a double portion in your land, and everlasting joy will be yours."* Not only had I received a new sense of self-worth, a stable, healthy mood, and an awareness of His goodness and mercy, but everything that I had grieved, everything that had been stolen from me, would now be redeemed! The depths of my pain, insanity, and deeply-embedded shame would now be the substance supernaturally transformed into a divine and bountiful inheritance.

As the course continued, I was asked to write letters to all those towards whom I harboured anger, including my boyfriend at the time, the nurses, doctors, and the legal system for the fact that abortion was so easily accessible to me in the first place.

The hardest chapter came when I finally connected with my precious daughter, Abigail Grace. I talked to her regularly and imagined her at the same age as my students, full of life. I experienced profound grace in this time as I trusted she was in Heaven cheering me on, but it was also heartbreaking to fully realize the consequences of my decision. At the end of the process, I had to let her go.

Today, I walk in freedom and in boldness, having removed the cloak of shame and guilt as expressed through mental instability and emotional dysregulation. What's more, I have total access to God. I no longer hold up the abortion as proof of my unworthiness; instead, I experience it as evidence of His deep, unfailing love and mercy. I am not hiding in the shadows, desperate to be accepted and understood; I am reconciled to the Father and restored as a proud mom—a woman empowered to live with joy and hope for the promise of what awaits her, both in this life and throughout eternity.

fifteen

One Love

by Mario

My story is not easy to tell, and may not be one you would like to hear, but it is about hope. The hope not found in things, or others, or even self. It's about the Living Hope that brings freedom, love, and victory and that produces courage and real joy.

My name is Mario, born in El Salvador into a family with Christian values and loving parents. Born to blessings that every child wants to have when growing up—parents who love you and take the time to nurture you and teach you about life from early childhood until it is time to leave home. Parents who truly care.

I came to Canada in the 90s. It took a while to settle and learn a new language and culture, but now Canada is home and, in my opinion, one of the best countries on the planet. My life throughout high school was normal, what any teenager would want and expect. However, at the age of seventeen, my desires and expectations changed, and all the values and counsel that my parents had poured into me went out the window. I became very self-centred, selfish, and arrogant.

In 1995, I met a friend who eventually became my best friend, then girlfriend, fiancée, and spouse. We had a very up-and-down relationship, even through our marriage. A big part of the problem stemmed from something that happened when we were dating that quietly haunted us into our marriage. My girlfriend got pregnant and we made the decision to abort our babies. Yes, I said babies because we found out they were twins.

We carried the decision we'd made about our babies deep in our hearts and never discussed or mentioned it. The decision to terminate the pregnancy had made sense to us at the time, and no one had the right to question that, as far as we were concerned. Little did we know how wrong we were.

My wife and I got married in 1999. We hadn't planned or decided that was the year we both wanted to tie the knot. The decision was made in a rush and in the fear of our parents finding out we were expecting again. This time we had decided to go through with the pregnancy and make our relationship work. Looking back, it was a foolish reason to rush into marriage, and that proved to be true as nothing went right, and I mean nothing. After we were finally married and at home with our first baby, everything should have been wonderful. Instead, our marriage was scarred by guilt and a post-abortion syndrome that caused our relationship to be damaged in every possible way.

By 2001, we had separated and within months we were divorced. Our parents and friends were devastated. Apparently, everyone had looked up to us because we looked so good together and had the appearance of this young lovely couple. Even though it may have appeared so, that was not the case within the walls of our home and in our secret hearts. It was a wrong view to have of us and a deceiving portrayal of our marriage relationship.

Our lives moved in separate directions. There was no hope of reconciliation or any attempt to restore our relationship. During the winter season of 2005, I found myself empty, confused, hopeless, stressed, and broken. No words could describe the state of my life because of the poor choices I was making. I was immersed in drugs, alcohol, the pursuit of worldly success, and sexual immorality. I believed so many lies that seemed to be true at the time.

Still, I was continually reminded of the counsel my parents had given me when I was growing up. I began asking God to show me if

He truly existed, and if He did, to show Himself in specific ways. And He did! I came to know Jesus and experienced redemption. My ex-wife also came to know her Saviour. These miracles were the result of the commitment of many believers to pray for us over the years, that we would be saved in Christ and our marriage would be restored for the glory of our awesome God and Father.

In the spring of 2005, God forgave us, saved us, and restored us back to himself, and we gave our lives to Christ. Our marriage was restored and our second child was born. It was quite a journey, and we were awed and amazed to see all that God had done in such a short time.

Three years into our remarriage, my wife asked me one night if I would seek counsel with her regarding the devastating decision that we had made about our babies. The first thought in my mind was, *why would I want to go through that when it is such a painful part of our past?* Little did I know then that I was in for some work to be done in my heart.

As a result of the conviction that the Spirit of God brought to her heart, my wife decided to enroll in a Christian pregnancy support services program in our city. She had been carrying shame, unforgiveness, anger, unbelief, and guilt in silence for many years. I teared up when she explained the program in detail and asked if I would support her. Immediately I said yes, not only because my best friend was asking me, and because of what I had gone through with her, but also because my eyes were opened and I saw the sin I had committed and the grief I had caused my heavenly Father.

Save One by Sheila Harper is a men's study that helped me to dealt with the guilt, anger, grief, and shame I had carried deep inside me and refused to talk about for many years. Through the study, I was able to face those feelings and work through them in a healthy way. The symptoms associated with Post-Abortion Stress Syndrome, or PAS, had been the strongholds of my heart. I harboured unresolved guilt regarding the abortion of my babies, because I had not said anything to anyone or asked for help. I had suppressed the truth about abortion by denying that it was wrong. I re-experienced the abortion through flashbacks whenever an advertisement against abortion was televised, posted, or mentioned. I would often think of God punishing me for the murder of my babies. I remembered the anniversary of the abortion without emotion or feeling. For many years, I was blinded by the deception and numbed by the sin I had committed.

On a deep level, the guilt of murdering my babies beat me up and led me to a place of doubting the promises of God. Many times I tried to deny and excuse the immoral choice I had made about my kids, but I suppressed my guilt. I did not want to talk about it or take responsibility for what I had done.

Another result of the PAS was my anger. The rage inside my heart was like a wave that would rise up and out of me and then retreat again to just below the surface, always threatening to overflow. It would come and go, inciting outbursts when I saw parents with twins or even pictures of families. Like a volcano, my anger would explode and vomit, not lava, but the harshest words towards my best friend and my children. The questions in the study led me to a place where I finally understood where my anger was coming from.

Grieving the loss of my babies was also part of the study. The suffering I had endured for many years in silence had to be dealt with. The hidden sorrow had impacted my life and put a strain on my marriage. I could not bring the twins back and make time and space right.

Through the study, I discovered the difference between guilt and shame. I learned that guilt says, "I made a mistake" and shame says, "I *am* a mistake." Both guilt and shame affected me and had been eating away at the core of my heart. Only heartfelt repentance could replace the guilt—I needed to accept and believe that my Saviour had paid for my sin and forgiven me. The shame from Satan's condemnation had to be replaced by the reality that I was forgiven and cleansed by Jesus.

I'm not saying that it was easy and accomplished overnight. The process took time and courage as I worked to uncover and share what the accuser was up to, that he had been constantly beating me up for all the poor choices I had made. But the living hope found in Christ Jesus is the hope that says to guilt, shame, sorrow, anger, distress, and hopelessness: "Hit the road!" Hope in Christ brings freedom, love, and victory.

The freedom Christ offers comes when He removes all our past, present, and future sins. He paid the price we owed for our sins on the cross out of love for you and me. Our sin debt was paid for in a single sacrifice through the shedding of His blood, making all who believe in Him clean and pure before our Father who is Holy. As it says in Hebrews 12:2b, *"For the joy set before him he endured the cross, scorning its shame, and sat down at the right hand of the throne of God."* In 1 Peter 2:9, He declares us a *"chosen people, a royal priesthood, a holy nation, God's special possession,"* so that we can proclaim his excellence and shine light and hope into this dark world.

His love! Man, where do I begin? Well, that word *love* is thrown around a lot. We say things like, "I love chocolate" or "I love that team." Countless songs have been written about supposed true love. One in particular I can think of has the phrase *one love,* but to that I say there is only one true love that covers over a multitude of sins as Peter describes in 1 Peter 4:8. The unconditional love shown by God to us in that, *while we were still sinners,* He showed His love for us, according to Romans 5:8.

When someone does something truly sacrificial for us, our instinct is to ask why. Only one answer nails it—God doesn't *do* love, He *is* love. And everything He does is a result of who He is.

Pause and think for a second. Who in their right mind would look at me, at the terrible choice I made to take life away, and love me just the way I am? I come with sin, fears, failures, shame, guilt, sorrow, and the list goes on. But Jesus, He has accomplished the great exchange—life in place of death, forgiveness for my sins in place of the wrath of Almighty God.

"For all have sinned and fall short of the glory of God" (Romans 3:23). The fact that I fell short of the glory of God because of my poor choice in not keeping my babies led me to death. As it says in Romans 6:23, *"For the wages of sin is death, but the gift of God is eternal life in Christ Jesus our Lord."* But He showed up when I asked Him, and He will do the same for you because He has promised that if we believe in Him, our sins will be wiped out. *"If you declare with your mouth, 'Jesus is Lord,' and believe in your heart that God raised him from the dead, you will be saved"* (Romans 10:9). God's promises are true and His love is true, redeeming love.

This kind of love leads to victory. In this victory, you and I experience grace upon grace. This grace is something you and I don't deserve, don't understand, and can't ultimately grasp. But His grace is sufficient for every temptation and difficulty in our daily tasks and circumstances. This is extremely important because the accuser will come and bring the shame, guilt, and sorrow back into our minds when you and I are most vulnerable.

> When sorrow over the decision to abort our babies threatens to overwhelm me, I claim those promises, and I find comfort and peace in the grace and mercy of God.

That's why our Victor has fought the fight. He brings the victory to us through His faithful Spirit and His true promises. He will never forsake us or forget us, rather, *"… to all who did receive him, to those who believed in his name, he gave the right to become children of God…"* (John 1:12). When sorrow over the decision to abort our babies threatens to overwhelm me, I claim those promises, and I find comfort and peace in the grace and mercy of God.

The facts or events, thoughts or mistakes, in our daily lives are not a surprise to God. He knows them all, cares about them all, and wants our hearts to belong to Him. After all, He created us. He simply invites us to live by faith, *"In order that in the coming ages he might show the incomparable riches of his grace, expressed in his kindness to us in Christ Jesus. For it is by grace you have been saved, through faith—and this is not from yourselves, it is the gift of God..."* (Eph. 2:7-8).

Life is a gift, and no matter how many how often we mess it up by our behaviours and choices, God is sovereign over all of it. He is love and our sins are covered by the forgiveness and mercy he offers us in Christ Jesus through the Holy Spirit. Our seconds, minutes, hours, days, months, and years are in the palm of His hand. He wants us to choose Him, to accept this gift of peace in Him.

Now is the time to embrace everything He has to offer us—life, forgiveness, freedom, love, and victory in the midst of our fears, anxieties, and wrongdoings. Whatever happened in our past, He will redeem and use it all if our hearts are set on Him. Christ knows our every thought and every desire even before we ask him.

Surrender your fears, failures, and sorrows to the Living Hope, Jesus Christ, and let your heart take hold of and share in the wonderful deeds He is doing. May you choose to live to the glory of our Father and be blessed beyond measure.

sixteen

The Sleeping Monster

by Hilarie Forkheim

I was twenty-four, he was twenty-eight. We'd been involved in a five-year relationship that started when we met at the office. A long-awaited engagement had eventually occurred, but his fear of committing to a wedding date had led me to break the relationship off and return the ring. That spiraled us into an "on and off" pattern.

Neither of us was happy together, yet we couldn't seem to stay apart. Currently we were "off", but clearly that hadn't been the case for long, because the call I'd received from the doctor's office that spring day in 1981 had just confirmed I was pregnant.

Fear, raw and panicked, gripped me. How could this be happening to me? What would people think or say about me? There was no way I could do this alone, and there was absolutely no way I was going to call him and tell him about it.

The only person I felt I could reach out to for counsel, comfort, and support was my oldest sister. Only it didn't happen like I imagined it would. I called her all right, but what I got was a big dose of shame and disgust. "Get to the doctor and get rid of it," was her terse advice.

That was it. Decision made, appointment made, and then it was over. I remember a few of the details—the doctor's jowled face as he sat behind his big wooden desk, the hospital location, but little else. Who picked me up? How did I feel afterward, physically, emotionally?

Things drifted back to normal. I went to work. I played slow pitch and broke my jaw taking a line drive to the face. And then he was back in my world, driving my car home while I went to the hospital and picking me up after my surgery.

In that window of reconnection, once the swelling went down in my wired jaw, I told him I had aborted our baby. There was no discussion, no reaction other than a nod of his head, simple acceptance. Not even a paragraph of sentences between us. He looked relieved. Subject closed. We finally had what we needed to make our drifting apart permanent—shame and relief.

Two years later, I had a new guy in my life. We had gone through the same relationship on and offs as I had with my previous boyfriend, but right now we were "on" and I sported a ring on my left hand. With a wedding date just five weeks away, I had everything I wanted.

And then the repeat phone call came from my doctor. I was pregnant—again! How could that be? He didn't want "it." It was too soon. His dad had died a few months prior and it was all too much to deal with, given his still-fresh grief and the stress of the upcoming wedding. At least that's what he told me, and I accepted it. I didn't call my sister this time. I kept my shame to myself.

I sat across the same wooden desk from the same jowled doctor. This time, he must have sensed something in my voice, some hesitancy. It made him stop filling out the required paperwork and look up at me. He paused, pen in hand, and asked if I had changed my mind.

I quickly assured him that I wasn't changing my decision, but that I felt guilty for doing this a second time. He picked up his pen and resumed his writing. But inside I was not certain at all. How I wished he would have put the pen down, really looked at the person in front of him, and had a different conversation. But he didn't and the cycle repeated.

I showed up for the required pre-treatment the day before the procedure, endured the shame of not just one doctor examining me but an intern as well. Snippets of the next day's procedures are there, the IV going in, waiting in the room, but not much else. I remember being at home in my apartment later with my fiancé. It was February 14, 1983. There were no flowers, no card, no chocolates—seriously?

And I had to practically beg him to go the store for the pads I needed for my recovery. That was it. It was over. But I was angry, and I resented what I perceived in him as cowardice. We never discussed it again. The wedding came and went. We lasted about a year, and then I found myself divorced for the first time. A typical outcome for a couple that aborts.

The years rolled by and I cycled through relationships with the certainty that whatever one I was currently in would be "the one" to last with permanency. Most were nice men, with respectable jobs, lives, and families. If I had a do-over with two of them there would be charges of date rape and undoubtedly jail time, but I didn't speak up.

Finally, in 1987, I met a good man I believed I could build a life with, and I married again in 1989. A year later, I began a degree program at the university. Life was pretty good, but not wanting to recreate the marriage my parents had, I also started counselling. I wanted my marriage to be successful and our future enjoyable. It wasn't my first venture into self-examination, but it was probably the most important.

One of the first things my counsellor warned me of was the significant impact counselling might have on my marriage in potentially negative ways. As I did the work to discover and accept myself, I would no longer be the same woman my husband married. He might not like that. He didn't. In the spring of 1991, during my second year of university, I got the shock of yet another birth control fail and my third unplanned pregnancy.

This time there was no question that I would see it through. I wasn't even sure I wanted kids, but still I embraced the prospect with excitement. I hadn't realized that part of me had been holding my breath. They tell you when you abort that it could impact your ability to conceive in the future. So, in an odd way I was relieved to know I still could. But the marriage was starting to show cracks, and I worried about bringing a child into our environment. We started couple's counselling right away and carried on for the next twenty-two months. Even though it changed me significantly, it couldn't save our union. We separated just after our daughter's first birthday.

At the age of thirty-five, I found myself a single mom with a baby, smack in the middle of my degree program. I had virtually no money in the bank and an ex-husband who wanted me to quit school. When I look back, that's not so different a position from where I was in my twenties facing pregnancy without a lot of security. Only this time I had the baby in tow, and I survived.

I finished my degree (with Distinction), raised my daughter jointly with her dad, worked my job, and enjoyed a full life with friends. How I wish someone had come alongside me in those early years to coach me about how doable—hard, but doable—keeping and raising a baby could be. I was so young and naïve to what other possibilities existed. If only I had known that help was available.

In the first few years after graduation, I had more time to reflect on life and what I wanted my future to look like. I took a course to help me work through some of the feelings and consequences of divorce with others going through the same experience. I discovered clues about my patterns and gained tools for setting boundaries and making better relational decisions. I continued to have relationships, fewer and more serious in nature than in my single days, but nothing seemed to stick.

Not that I didn't have wonderful men coming into my life during this time, but I always seemed to be yearning for that missing something. As a result, I systematically ended each relationship. On good terms, but I ended them, nonetheless.

I started to wonder about more things than ever and turned to God for answers. I didn't know much about God, but I believed he was there. One day while out for a run, I was gazing up into the clouds talking to him in my head. I had recently ended a live-in relationship and asked God for a sign about what to do next. As I refocused my sight on the path in front of me, I nearly collided with a sandwich board on the sidewalk. It was an invitation to a church being held in a near-by movie theatre. Well, okay then. Not only did God have a sense of humour by literally providing a sign, he answered me very promptly.

My daughter and I started attending the little church soon after and quickly learned about God's forgiving and loving nature. I read in the Bible that if we bring the things we've done that are against his moral code, and apologize sincerely, he is faithful not only to forgive us our wrongdoings, but also to purify us from all we've done to harm ourselves and others. I wanted to enjoy the full benefits of a relationship with him, so I made a list of all my regrets and brought them to him, including my two abortions. I felt his compassion and the freedom from the weight of my poor choices and sorrows.

The Bible also says that God's unfailing love for those who choose him is as great as the height of the heavens above the earth *and* that he removes our mistakes from us as far as the east is from the west. And that is exactly the freedom I felt. I started to live life differently. Relationships with men became less of a focus, and I became part of a church community that supported me in friendship and in discovering a more rewarding purpose in life. I began to pray for a like-minded husband, and two years later, he showed up. I married for a third time and suddenly had three daughters instead of just one.

Being remarried provided me the opportunity to stay home with the girls and engage fully in the difficult work of blending a family. It also gave me time to start volunteering. My first placement was with an agency that offered assistance to those facing unplanned pregnancies or experiencing post-abortion stress. Then I added the role of facilitating conversation with a small group of single moms through our church once a month. And not long after that, I became part of a team organizing annual retreats that provided women the opportunity for quiet inner reflection. It was at those retreats that I began to encounter women with long-standing abortion stress. I was a safe place to instigate healing conversations before they moved on to others more qualified to counsel women with these wounds.

A few years into these volunteer activities, a guest speaker for women in leadership at church spoke on the effects of abortion. The purpose of the talk was to prepare us for the likely event that we would meet someone who needed to talk about it. She explained that, statistically, most women feel relief after an abortion, but denial of other, more powerful emotions is hard to maintain forever. She went on to say that grief over an abortion can often surface years or even decades later, manifesting itself in many destructive ways. She noted that the root struggle for women lay in forgiving themselves. And that's when I realized that while God had forgiven me, something I knew to my core, I wasn't so sure I had forgiven myself. Together with one of the women I had spoken to about abortion at a retreat, I engaged in a post-abortion recovery group. This required me to take another look at my own stories and the impact my two abortions had really had on my life.

> And that's when I realized that while God had forgiven me, something I knew to my core, I wasn't so sure I had forgiven myself.

I dove into this self-examination experience in earnest. It was a deeper, more honest, more vulnerable dive than I'd ever done before. And it was during this process of healing that my eyes were opened to the impact of a long-ago occurrence. It wasn't that I had forgotten about it, it was simply that I hadn't attributed the proper perspective or importance to what had happened that it deserved. I didn't realize that all these years later it was a key to so many of my decisions in life, especially to how quickly and easily I had chosen to abort—twice.

I was molested at age six. One of the milestone developments of a six-year-old is being able to speak in complete sentences with five to seven words. How then could I be expected to understand any form of sexual activity with the perpetrator—another child, someone I loved and who loved me—let alone consent to it? It was so confusing. An unexpected game I was coerced into. It didn't feel right. My six-year-old self believed "I did something bad." Without the vocabulary, I didn't know that what I felt was fear, shame, and guilt. And like every kid that doesn't want to get into trouble, I didn't tell anyone. Even if I could have mustered the courage to bring it up, how would I have explained what had happened?

Soon we moved to a new province, and in the chaos of that transition, no one noticed the change in me, that I had shut down. The threat of more encounters was removed, and life went on. But the impact of the offence had a lasting and devastating effect on me. The message "you do not get to decide what happens to your body, others do" had been planted deep inside of me and it laid in wait until puberty and capitalizing boys came along.

The first time a boy held my hand, it was as if I had been hit by a bolt of lightning from my head to my toes. It was shocking and overwhelming. But I couldn't say *stop* because I wasn't in charge of my body. As the years progressed, the touching did too, and by sixteen I was having intercourse. I didn't enjoy it, not at all. It sickened me, but I couldn't stop it. If I wanted "love" from a guy, this dissociating and freezing—that is to say, not stopping the sexual advances—was the price I had to pay for it. Not until many years later was there any pleasure in it. But still I wasn't in control of my body, men were.

At age eighteen, when I started work in a downtown corporate office, I was vulnerable to the charms of someone five years older than me. I was flattered that he was interested in me. He took me for nice dinners and to the theatre. He bought me long-stemmed, red roses. They were boxed with a beautiful red bow, and he bought them for me often. He presented me with nice gifts. He was generous and a romantic. It wasn't until well into the relationship that he disclosed that he had targeted me for a relationship because he knew I was "experienced." He lied about a supposed back injury that kept him from normal performance in the early going. But the truth was, he was a nervous virgin, and he used me to show him the ropes. By the time we broke off our engagement and started into the on-off relational cycle, two of his friends had taken the opportunity to sleep with me during the offs. I mean hey, they knew what they could get if they pretended they cared about me, right?

The mountain of shame grew with each physical encounter, so when I found myself single and pregnant, the cherry on the top of the crowning shameful event of my life was served up by my own sister. The fastest way to distance myself from the shame, as far as I was concerned, was to abort and make the problem go away. That's why I didn't tell him. It was bad enough that my sister knew and shamed me. I wasn't going to let him do it too.

And the second abortion went much the same. We kept it quiet; it was my problem, my shame—not his, mine. I was angry, but I wanted to be loved so badly that I stuffed it all deep inside and kept a lid on it. Life carried on, and while I had my regrets, felt bad for what I'd done, I wasn't plagued by guilt. It didn't stop me from progressing in my jobs, getting an education, marrying and having a family, taking vacations, and generally living my life. But there was a sleeping monster inside of me that would need to be faced one day, and at the age of fifty, the post-abortion recovery group provided me with the opportunity I needed.

In that group, I began to understand that God had long ago forgiven me for terminating those two pregnancies. That was His piece of work with me. But I also began to understand that I had yet to do my piece with Him. The piece that would ultimately bring freedom from the shame of what I had done and why. I had no idea how much I needed that course and the women who completed it with me.

From the young women, one of whom was just two weeks post-abortion and very raw, to the two of us old-timers, we all helped each other. I learned how to say hello to my babies and then say good-bye. The discovery of who I was then, and who I am now, is an ongoing process. The repressed grief of my abortions has impacted every aspect of my life—my self-confidence, employment, friendships, finances, parenting, marriage, and so much more. I just hadn't seen that before.

In the twelve years since completing the program, I have continued to uncover more layers of what I call the lost years and accept them as part of me. I think if I had uncovered them all at once, it would have destroyed me. Grieving is a process. It stays with you, but it doesn't need to own you. Life, and a good one at that, can carry on.

I know that God is good, and He is patient. His Word promises compassion for those who call on his name, and that he will restore the lost years and fortunes. And *that* is something worth holding on to. There's so much more to my story, but the bottom line is that once the door to truth has been opened, there is hope and healing ahead for me and those who have experiences like mine. I'm so glad that I stepped through it!

seventeen

Yeshu – Please Help

by Jayne Barthorpe

After leaving Canada and arriving in Australia two days later, I thought my mother might greet this travel-weary birthday girl with acceptance, if not warmth. But as I pulled open the sliding door and popped my head inside, what I got was a finger pointing at me and the words, "No Jesus talk, Jayne!"

My heart sank at the coldness of the greeting and the sight of her with an oxygen tube attached to her nose and trailing behind her.

That was February 10, 2017.

Two months later, everything changed.

"Yeshu. Yeshu, please help me. Yeshu. Yeshu, please help me." This was my ninety-three-year-old mother's call throughout the day on Tuesday, April 18th.

Sitting on a chair in the lounge of my parents' home, I asked her, "Mom, do you need help? Who are you calling to?"

She gestured with her hands for me to go away.

Tubes flowing from her nose to the oxygen tank beside her, struggling to draw in breaths, she continued to call out, "Yeshu, please help me."

My heart did a somersault as I perceived her words. Was she calling out to Yeshua-Jesus? For over four decades I had been praying for the salvation of my parents, sharing the gospel of Jesus Christ many times. Over the years my children and grandchildren, as well as other brothers and sisters in Christ, had joined me in prayer for them.

When they both reached ninety, I became more concerned and burdened for them, as time was truly closing in.

My middle daughter Sarah reassured me that this passion to pray for their salvation daily was of God, and He would not place this on us if there was no hope.

We persevered in prayer even as they repeatedly rejected hearing about God's redemption plan. My heart's cry was that an ambulance assistant, a nurse, a doctor, or any medical professional who was a believer, would be faithful to share the gospel with my parents, as their physical needs increased. Perhaps they would listen to someone like that, if they wouldn't listen to us. Over and over we prayed fervently that the Lord would show them their need for Him and that He would grant them the gift of repentance and salvation in Him.

At about 8:30 that Tuesday evening, after her calling out to Yeshu throughout the day, my ninety-five-year-old dad and I helped Mom to the bedroom.

I sat on the edge of the bed, observing her and reflecting quietly on the day, my father beside me. Suddenly my mother blurted out, "Jayne, I've sinned!"

Joy flooded through me. I'd been telling my parents that truth for years, but their reply had always been the same, "We are good people." My heart had broken over that, because how can anyone accept and receive a Saviour they don't believe they need?

I couldn't stop the smile that crossed my face as I reached for her hand. "Mom, we've all sinned, I'm also a sinner; that's why God sent His Son Jesus. On the cross He suffered beyond our human thinking, taking the just punishment from God for sin—our sin, all of it, past, present, and future."

"Jayne, you don't understand, I have a big sin."

I shook my head. "Mom, no sin is too big for Jesus to forgive. He can and will forgive you, but first you must believe in Jesus and know that He suffered and died on the cross for our sins, and that on the third day He rose and, yes, today He is alive. Then, with sorrow in our hearts over our sin, we can confess them to Him and ask Jesus to forgive us."

Mom nodded. "Yes, yes. I want to do that!"

I started to respond, but Mom wasn't done. "I had an abortion in 1956, sixty-one years ago. A boy."

Suddenly I was having as much trouble taking a breath as my mother. I'd had a fourth brother? Shock froze me in place. *God help me; give me the words to say.* Peace came over me as I held my mother's hand. "Mom, that little baby, your son, he's in heaven with Jesus."

Dad spoke up, his voice stern. "Jayne, what your mother said is not true. She is on heavy medication; she is not speaking the truth." Dad said these words several times, but somehow they did not register with me at the time. If they had, I might not have said what I did, so I believe the Holy Spirit was protecting His plan, which was about to unfold.

I turned back to Mom. "You said you want to give your sins—all your sins including the abortion of your baby boy—to Jesus and ask Him for His forgiveness?"

"Yes. Yes!" Mom said with urgency in her voice.

I then led my Mom in a deep, sorrowful prayer to Jesus, asking Him to forgive her of the many decades of sin as well as the sin of abortion, to wash her *"white as snow"* as it says in Isaiah 1:18 and Psalm 51:7, and to remove those sins from her *"as far as the east is from the west,"* as God promised to do in Psalm 103:12.

I shared with her those words of truth from Scripture. God's words of assurance. Wow!

Then, and a big then, I took her thin, vein-lined hand in both of mine and said to her, "Mom, since you've put your belief and trust in Jesus to forgive you of all your life's sins, knowing what He endured on the cross to pay for your sins and acknowledging the power of

God that raised Him, wouldn't you like to accept Jesus as your Lord and your Saviour by asking Him into your heart and into your life?"

What happened next is one of the greatest gifts in my life. Without hesitation, my Mom said, "Yes, please!"

My dad had quieted down, and I prayed he was listening to all that was being said. Mom and I bowed our heads and Mom confessed that she believed in Jesus, believed that He endured through intense suffering, died on the cross to pay for our sins, rose from the dead on the third day, and is alive today, presently seated at the right hand of our one true God on the throne in heaven.

My mother's beautiful prayer—and her realization that she was a sinner in need of a Saviour—was the answer to decades of prayer. Hallelujah, praise our King. Thank you, Jesus! My mom was now saved from eternal death. Jesus Christ gets all the praise and glory.

By this time, Mom was physically and mentally exhausted from the day, so Dad and I put her to bed.

Dad, clearly moved and overwhelmed by all that had just happened, also went off to bed.

I spent the night praising my King Jesus for my mother's salvation and also that He had actually chosen me to lead her to Him. I was overjoyed at the privilege and kindness of God to bless me in this way.

The next day, Mom shared with me that she had been calling, "Yeshu, please help me" in order to find the strength to tell me about her 'sinful abortion' in 1956.

Mom had been in bondage to this sin for sixty-one years. She was now free; her chains had been broken, according to Hebrews 2:15. Praise King Jesus.

Then Wednesday the 19th came. Philippians 4:7 says, "And the peace of God, which surpasses all understanding, will guard your hearts and minds in Jesus Christ."

I was so very blessed to see that truth revealed through my mom's demeanour that Wednesday. She had finally brought her secret into the healing light. She had experienced the relief of confessing it to me and to her Creator. She had taken hold of the free gift of forgiveness and had been brought into a place of peace with the Eternal God of the universe. She was no longer separated from Him by her sin. No longer under condemnation, she was free! I could literally see that the weight of years of bondage, and consequently bitterness, had dropped from her as though a heavy cloak had been removed. I was deeply grieved that she had been held in fear and captivity by the enemy for sixty-one years but also greatly relieved and thankful for God's miraculous plan of salvation that had unfolded before me.

The day was filled with absolute calmness. As Mom experienced peace with God and comfort from forgiveness, she breathed slowly and steadily, with the aid of the oxygen, as she sat dozing in the lounge chair.

On the other hand, my dad was very quiet, keeping to himself. Obviously quite restless, he busied himself in his woodwork shop, constantly in and out of the house.

I know he was concerned about his beloved wife's health, as they had been close companions for over seven decades.

I puttered about making cups of tea, lunch, then later supper for my dad and myself. Mom at this stage was hardly eating.

At 7:30 pm, I walked Mom to the bedroom. We paused below an archway between the lounge/dining room area and their main bedroom. I looked at her and said, "Mom, you've had a wonderful day, you've been so calm and peaceful."

Mom patted my hand. "Oh Jayne, I have no words to describe the peace I feel."

I replied, "Mom, that's the peace of Jesus, and only He can give you that."

My joy in seeing a new creation when I looked at Mom was indescribable. Paul says in 2 Corinthians 5:17: "*Therefore, if anyone is in Christ, the new creation has come. The old has gone, the new is here!*"

Even though her spirit was reborn, her physical body was deteriorating, and we knew she didn't have much time left with us. Her night was quite restless.

Thursday, April 20th arrived.

Dad and I enjoyed a quiet breakfast together, then he offered to do the breakfast dishes as I went off to take a shower and get dressed.

As I was making my bed and preparing for family to arrive, Dad rushed into the room. "Come quickly, Jayne, come quickly!" My immediate thought was that Mom had taken a bad turn, so I rushed into the hallway after Dad.

When we reached the dining room, my dear Papa gestured to the table. "Sit quickly, your brother and his wife are arriving soon from South Africa."

I glanced up at the kitchen clock. "Dad, it's not even ten a.m. Their plane lands at noon, then they need to clear customs and collect their baggage."

I refrained from adding that my youngest brother was picking them up from the airport and bringing them to my parents' home, and it was about a ninety-minute drive from the airport. It was unlikely they would arrive before two that afternoon, four hours from now.

Dad shook his head emphatically. "No, sit quickly."

Like an obedient—if almost seventy-year-old daughter—I sat down and so did Dad.

Dad sat upright as he always did, his hands fidgeting on the table. "What your mother said on Tuesday evening about having an abortion, it is all true. I helped her to abort our baby boy; I have also sinned." Tears filled his eyes.

My throat tightened. The last time I had seen my dad cry was sixty years ago, in 1957, when he received news from England that his mother had passed away.

His eyes still filled with tears, Dad, restless and clearly needing to talk, said, "I also want to do what your mother did."

I studied my dad's sad face. "You want to ask Jesus to forgive you for the abortion sin and all your other sins?"

"Yes. Yes," was his reply.

I leaned closer. "And you want to ask Jesus into your heart, to be your Saviour and Lord of your life?"

"Yes. Yes. Yes," he repeated.

There was a definite urgency in his voice, and his emotions were running high.

I then spoke to my dad with what felt like the authority of the Holy Spirit. "Dad, this is a very serious matter, a commitment to Jesus. I don't want you to simply copy what Mom did if your heart does not believe; it must be *your* heart's conviction and desire."

Dad pressed the palms of his hands to the table. "Yes, yes, yes, that's what I want."

So we held hands and bowed our heads, and I received a second great gift from God. I led my dear dad in a prayer asking forgiveness for his life's sins as well as his involvement in the abortion of his baby boy. Dad repeated what I said word for word. We prayed for Jesus to live within his heart as he confessed that he believed in the finished work of Jesus on his behalf. I listened with wonder as my dad proclaimed that Jesus is alive!

Jesus was now my dad's Lord and Saviour. I praise King Jesus for His amazing grace; where once my dad was blind, he now saw very clearly.

To those of you reading this story now, I offer you these words of assurance from my heart. Jesus died for all our sins, past, present, and future. Sin is sin; we cannot categorize it into 'small' or 'big.'

If you have not already done so, take your sins to Him and ask for His forgiveness. You do not need to live your life in bondage to your sin, a slave to it. Give it to Jesus. He paid a heavy price for our sins on the cross so that we could be free.

Secondly, never give up on prayers for the salvation of your loved ones—family members, friends, and neighbours. Salvation happens in His perfect timing, as it did for my parents after over four decades of prayer for them, for the softening of their hearts and the realization that they were sinners.

Now, all the praise and glory goes to our precious Lord and Saviour, Jesus Christ.

Wow. My head was spinning. What amazing days I had just lived through, with my parents realizing they were actually sinners in need of a Saviour, then both of them praying for the forgiveness of their decades of sins, including entrusting that the shed blood of Jesus on Calvary was enough to pay the penalty for killing their baby boy so long ago.

They were finally free after sixty-one years of living in secret guilt and bondage. I only wish they had not waited so long to be freed to live in the love, joy, and abundant life that walking with Jesus brings. Don't wait, beloved, today is the day of your salvation.

> You do not need to live your life in bondage to your sin, a slave to it. Give it to Jesus.

I saw an immediate transformation in both of them. At the ages of ninety-three and ninety-five, they were experiencing the miracle of regeneration, of new life!

Family arrived in time to be at Mom's side as she lay in the hospital bed that had been brought into my parents' home for her. On Friday she deteriorated further, her breathing growing increasingly laboured.

The nursing staff came in and put her on morphine, and from then on she became non-responsive.

She was surrounded by family and a few close friends. The Navy chaplain also visited us, as arranged by the Silver Chain care group. The chaplain prayed over Mom and prayed for the family too.

Saturday, April 22nd came. It felt like a long, slow day with medical folks coming to see Mom and administer more morphine. Again, the Navy chaplain came to visit Mom and the family, praying once more. Dad, surrounded by family, had our support. He stayed by her side virtually constantly.

Then, at ten past six, as the sun was setting on that day, my mom took her last breath. She stepped peacefully into eternity and felt the embrace of nail-scarred hands.

My dad, my youngest brother, and I were with her as she passed. No words can truly express what it was like to be with her in her very last moments on earth, knowing she was walking into the presence of the Lord.

Dad stayed with Mom, holding her hand, for a couple of hours, until the funeral home came to collect her. I slipped my arm through his and we waved good-bye to her.

After Mom was taken away, Dad gathered all his family together and said, "I have a request to make: please can we all go to church together in the morning?"

Silence descended over the room for a moment. This was totally unheard of. My dad had only ever gone to church for baby baptisms, weddings, and funerals. Now he was asking that we all go to church together.

On Sunday morning, April 23rd, I took my dad his early morning cup of tea and pulled back the curtains to reveal a beautiful sunny day with not a cloud in the sky. I was aware, though, that the cloud of loss would be thick and heavy in Dad's heart.

I rested my hand in his. "Dad, this is the first day you've woken up without your sweetheart next to you in over seven decades." I then quoted Psalm 118:24, "*This is the day that the LORD has made; let us rejoice and be glad in it*" (ESV).

I repeated the verse, this time slowly. Then I opened my Bible to that very passage and read it. When I finished, I held out my Bible. "Would you like to read it for yourself, Dad?"

His face lit up as he held my Bible for the first time and read the words that would become his strength over the next days.

My heart swelled at the sight. "Dad, Jesus loves to hear you speak Scripture out loud."

So, the Lord heard those verses four times. And then we went to a Sunday morning church service together, with my dad, for the first time in my life.

I decided to do a devotional each morning with my dad to start the day off with our 'cuppa.' Over the next eight months and one week, until he passed to be with Jesus and his sweetheart, we went through the Gospel of John a couple of times and many other Scriptures.

On Tuesday, April 25th, three days after Mom's passing, Dad asked me to accompany him to the funeral home to choose some hymns and prepare the order of service. As he drove, he glanced up at the beautiful, clear-blue sky and said, "Psalm 118, verse 24. '*This is the day that the LORD has made; let us rejoice and be glad in it*'."

Wow. Joy coursed through me. This was the first Scripture verse my father had ever memorized, and he did it at ninety-five years of age. He even quoted the Scripture's address in the Bible. Amazing!

I would never again doubt the words of Matthew 19:26b, "... *with God all things are possible.*"

At Mom's celebration, several family members did readings, including one from John 14. Dad found so much comfort in verses two and three where Jesus told His disciples that, "*In My Father's house are many rooms; if it were not so, would I have told you that I go to prepare a place for you? And if I go and prepare a place for you, I will come again and will take you to myself, that where I am you may be also*" (ESV). Dad was comforted by the absolute assurance that Mom was in heaven with Jesus.

During the next few months, he memorized all those verses, including verse six, which I believe to be an important verse to show that Jesus is the only mediator between God and man. Jesus speaks to Thomas saying, "… I am the way and the truth and the life. No one comes to the Father except through Me."

During the eight months and one week that my dear dad was a Christian, he never missed coming with me to church any Sunday, unless he was in hospital. When that happened, he would re-read the daily devotionals we'd done together.

I had attended the Rockingham Baptist church on all my visits to Australia. Members of the congregation came alongside me in prayer for my parents, and they also visited them. After Mom passed, a gentleman named Ken came to visit and have fellowship with Dad while I attended a Wednesday afternoon ladies Bible study. Both Ken and his wife Trisha always welcomed Dad to church on Sundays, as did many others.

By November, I needed to return to Canada as it was getting much too hot for me in Australia, and I had been there ten months already. I assured my dad I'd be back in three months.

My youngest brother recorded a "good-bye" video from our dad in the hospital just days before he passed. In it, my dad talked of the great love he had for all of us, then he said, "Soon I'm going to be with Jesus and your mother." Those were the sweetest words ever!

At twenty to midnight on December 29th, 2017, I awoke and was prompted by the Holy Spirit to Skype Australia. It could only have been the Holy Spirit, as I normally phoned my brother to see how Dad was. My brother answered the Skype call on his iPad from the hospital where Dad had been taken.

Over the iPad, he showed me Dad. He told me that Dad was not doing well and that his eyes had been closed since the day before. I told my brother I wanted to talk to him, and he held the device close to Dad's face.

I said, "Hello Daaaad." His eyes opened and tears welled in my eyes. I said, "We all love you," and he nodded his head slightly. My throat tight, I added, "Jesus loves you, Dad." Again he nodded his head a little. I gripped the phone tightly. "Dad, soon, very soon, you'll see Jesus face to face." Again a small nod. "And you'll also see Mom." One final nod then his eyes closed again. About a minute later, his face completely relaxed. That was the moment he went to be with Jesus. Wow. What an amazing God we have to allow me the wonderful privilege of witnessing the very moment each of my parents literally stepped into eternity to meet their Jesus!

It's now been two years since my mom passed and sixteen months since Dad went to be with the Lord. Almost every day, since they accepted Jesus as their Lord and Saviour on April 18th and 20th, 2017, I thank my Jesus for His faithfulness, His answers to prayer, His loving kindness in setting those captives free, and for taking them to live with Him forever in perfect peace. I am eternally thankful for their salvation in Jesus Christ. I know without a doubt that they are both in heaven with God. I look forward to the day my Lord chooses to take me home to Him, where I will see and rejoice with my parents. And I very much look forward to wrapping my arms around my fourth beautiful brother whom I never met on earth.

Thank you for your loving kindness, my Jesus.

eighteen

Emotional Healing after Abortion

by Elizabeth A. Skidmore, Ph.D.

H er story was like many others:

"I had a young child, no money, I was pregnant and the baby's father was on his way to prison. What was I to do? *What was I to do?*" Years later she looked back on that time in her life and sighed. "It wasn't that I didn't want the baby, it's just that... what kind of life could I offer the child?"

An unwanted pregnancy can thrust a woman or young girl into a crisis situation in which none of the available options seems feasible or favourable. It is a terrible time of stress and uncertainty, with no easy answers. Feeling there is no way out, she may conclude that abortion is the best solution, even the only one. Reasons for this are deep and personal, and research shows most women choosing to terminate a pregnancy feel a sense of relief afterwards.

My placement in university was at Planned Parenthood, a local agency that provided information to women about contraception and abortion services. It was the only opportunity available in my community to actually garner experience in counselling. Hopefully, I would be able to help women see they had other options besides abortion for an unplanned pregnancy.

The goal was to ensure that women were making an "informed decision," had considered adoption, and were aware of community resources that would support them through pregnancy and childbirth.

There were many different ages, backgrounds, and reasons why women felt they couldn't support a pregnancy at that time; the vast majority had made up their minds long before they arrived for the appointment. Sitting with the distressed and nervous women, I could usually understand their reasoning—they believed having a baby would interrupt their schooling; ruin their reputation; shame the family; financially burden a family that already lacked resources; the women were too young to parent or were already overwhelmed by parenting existing children; the pregnancy was the result of sexual assault, etc. It was not my place to judge, just to have them sign off that they had been given the opportunity to learn about all available options.

Common Feelings Following Abortion

Major mental health issues after abortion are rare; however, there are some common feelings in the days and weeks following the procedure:

Guilt – Feeling guilty about the choices you made that resulted in the unplanned pregnancy and the subsequent choice of abortion.

Anger – Anger at the situation, yourself, or others, especially if the decision to terminate the pregnancy was forced on you by someone else.

Shame – Perceived need for secrecy and silence, lack of social support from others, and/or feelings of stigma.

Remorse or regret – Questioning your decision, wishing things had turned out differently.

Loss of self-esteem or self-confidence – Feeling poorly about yourself, viewing yourself negatively.

Feelings of isolation and loneliness – A pervasive sense that no one understands, not wanting to be around others or socialize.

Difficulty sleeping and bad dreams – Sleep challenges can range from difficulty falling asleep, staying asleep, or early morning awakening. Dream content can be troubling – dreaming about loss, the baby, the abortion procedure itself.

Relationship problems – Withdrawing from others, shutting down emotionally, acting out behaviourally.

Thoughts of death or suicide – Believing you don't deserve to live or be happy, that others might be better off without you, or that life isn't worth living. When fleeting suicidal thoughts linger and you develop a plan for ending your life, talk to someone immediately and ask for help. Call your doctor, visit an emergency room, or call 911 if you fear you might act on those impulses.

Choose to Heal

Sometimes problems emerge over time for women who initially handled the abortion well. These can be due to life events that remind you of the past pregnancy or reproductive issues such as becoming pregnant again; giving birth to a planned or wanted pregnancy; infertility; a friend's pregnancy and subsequent birth; or awakening introspection and spirituality in your own personal life. Wherever you are in the healing process, the following suggestions will help you on your way to emotional and spiritual freedom:

Start by acknowledging the abortion happened. This might sound strange, but there are a number of reasons why an individual might be living as though nothing ever happened. Sometimes when dealing with crisis situations, we feel as if we are moving on auto-pilot, emotionally removed from the situation as a way of protecting our hearts and minds. Emotional "stuffers" often suppress uncomfortable thoughts and feelings, which may lead the individual to feel calloused and hardened, detached or aloof, emotionally shut down, anxious and depressed, or numb.

In a quiet and safe environment, alone or with a person you trust, let the memories and feelings come; *feel them*. It is difficult work, but you can do it, especially with support. You may wish to write the memories in a journal that you keep in a confidential place. Be sure to include not just the details of the event itself, but how you were feeling at the time, as well as how you are feeling now as you write about it.

Break your silence. You don't have to suffer in silence or alone. Share with a trusted friend, spiritual leader, or professional what has happened, and be open to receive their love, support, and grace. This is not a time to blame others or yourself, it is time to face what has happened, allow yourself to feel the pain, and to receive the loving kindness and forgiveness that come from God, others, and ultimately yourself.

Embark on a healing journey. Make a loving commitment to yourself to stop avoiding the issue and do the hard work of processing the circumstances, thoughts, and emotions surrounding the decision process and termination of your pregnancy. Workbooks are available in book stores and online, and there may be groups for grief recovery, post-abortion adjustment, and trauma in your own community. Avoid "extreme" groups where you might feel pressured to think the way the group does and thus avoid being truly honest and open with yourself and God. A "safe" group will be one in which all members are welcome to share their opinions and experiences in a non-judgmental environment of encouragement and hope.

Find an accountability partner. This should be someone you trust, with whom you can be totally honest. A good accountability partner will listen more than offer advice, and can help you resist the urge to fall back into denial, avoidance, self-blame, and despair. Give this person permission to share with you any concerns they have about your physical and emotional health (especially if they are concerned you may be thinking about suicide) as you journey toward healing.

Say goodbye to your unborn child. This can be accomplished by writing a letter that you write and re-write until it says exactly what you would want the child to know. You can keep it in a safe place or destroy it, ensuring that no one will ever see it.

Consider having a ceremony to honour the unborn child. Some individuals like to light a candle, share readings of hope, ask for forgiveness, and/or release helium balloons as a loving goodbye. There may be a chaplain at your local hospital willing to have a private remembrance service for your child. Many individuals have found this helpful as a means of bringing closure to the experience.

Commit to looking forward in your life. Our window of opportunity for living life is *today*. Humble yourself and sincerely seek God's forgiveness for your past mistakes. Determine to make changes in your life that are consistent with positive mental and physical health. Look to God to lead you in a deeply rewarding and satisfying way that is pleasing to him. A verse that brings me hope is 2 Corinthians 5:17: *"Therefore, if anyone is in Christ, the new creation has come: The old has gone, the new is here!"*

Grief, Unresolved Grief, or Trauma

It is natural to feel a sense of loss and grief over ending a pregnancy and important to honestly and courageously face those feelings. For most women, natural healing will occur over time. However, certain groups of women are more likely to experience negative outcomes following abortion than others:

Young age – a woman's age at the time of abortion influences how she is likely to respond. Younger women are more at risk for poor emotional outcomes.

Previous history of depression or mental illness – women who have struggled with depression or another type of mental illness in the past are known to have more difficulty adjusting to the loss.

Feelings of coercion and attachment to the child – anger, resentment, and a sense of loss of control are common when someone else imposed the decision on the woman, while those who felt connected to the child are likely to feel a keener sense of loss.

Number of children the woman already has – the more children, the more difficult the adjustment.

Gestational age of the baby at time of termination – the further along a woman is in her pregnancy the harder it will be for her. This is particularly true for second and third trimester abortions.

Physical complications from the abortion – occasionally the physical healing process is complicated or difficult. Some women are unable to conceive again afterwards, leading to a profound sense of loss and regret.

Weakened coping skills – women who have difficulty coping with stress or who cope in maladaptive ways (drug or alcohol abuse, cutting, withdrawing emotionally) often find a terminated pregnancy taxes their already weakened ability to deal with their situations.

While severe psychological distress, post-abortion, is rare, higher rates of anxiety, depression, substance use, traumatic symptoms, sleep disorders, and other negative outcomes are known to exist among post-abortion women than in the general population. How do you know if you are experiencing normal grief or if you need help?

Grief is the experience of loss. It is normal to feel a sense of loss and grief following a terminated pregnancy. Don't expect to simply get up the next morning as though nothing emotional has happened. Take time to feel and express your feelings in safe and appropriate ways, such as those listed above. It's okay to feel down or a bit anxious afterward.

Unresolved grief is grief that goes on for a longer period of time than would normally be expected, given the circumstances. It is grief that doesn't seem to get better, possibly even interfering with a person's ability to take care of daily responsibilities. Sometimes referred to as "complicated grief," it can quietly morph into depression or anxiety. There is no set period of time after which we determine someone has unresolved grief; however, if you are still having troubling emotions after several months, it would be wise to reach out for help.

Trauma can be defined as an emotional response to an event or experience that is deeply distressing or disturbing. Many people experience traumatic events through the course of their lives, but not all individuals develop Post-traumatic Stress Disorder (PTSD). PTSD can be conceptualized as a problem in recovery—something has blocked the individual's road to natural recovery from trauma, and his or her avoidance of the situation (stuffed feelings, pretending nothing happened, and staying away from things or people that remind him or her of the traumatic event) keeps that individual stuck.

Symptoms of post-traumatic stress fall into four categories: 1) re-experiencing the event through flashbacks, nightmares, or unwanted thoughts or images; 2) avoidance of people or situations that remind you of the traumatic incident; 3) cognitive changes (changes in how you think) which include an alteration in the way you view yourself, others, and the world; and 4) physiological arousal, such as insomnia, irritability, difficulty concentrating, or feeling hyper-alert. PTSD is a treatable illness that requires fully processing the traumatic event and becoming aware of how you are thinking about it.

Healing comes when you understand how your thoughts about the event are impacting your emotions and ultimately your behaviours.

When to Seek Help

In general, if you are feeling "stuck" and everything in life just feels hard, you may need help. If you are having difficulty functioning at school, home, or work; engaging in self-defeating behaviours; or feeling suicidal, you definitely need to seek professional help. I often use the analogy of a quilt. At first the stressful or traumatic event seems to dominate the entire quilt – we look at our lives and that is all we see. As we do the difficult work of healing, however, the "trauma" quilt square begins to shrink and take its place among the other quilt squares of our life experiences and we can go on.

Accessing professional services can be daunting for the young, or those who lack finances for medical help or counselling. A good place to start might be your school psychologist, social worker, or family doctor, who may be able to refer you to community resources such as Teen Health Centres or walk-in mental health clinics affiliated with local hospitals. Some community mental health services provide free or reduced-cost counselling based on family income. Psychologists, social workers and psychotherapists in private practice may also offer reduced fees, if you request assistance. Don't be afraid to ask. Have your doctor recommend a professional who is knowledgeable about post-abortion adjustment.

My Story

One day my neighbour confided in me that she was unexpectedly pregnant with her fourth child. Distraught, she lamented that she was already overwhelmed by her full-time work schedule, a husband with a stressful job, and their three other children, one of whom was still a toddler. I flashed back to when my own children were very young and I had a pregnancy scare—a late period and rising panic as to how I could manage a third child, which prompted a call to my doctor. Fortunately, my period started the next day. My friend's situation turned out differently, but I could relate to her sense of fear, loss of control, and helplessness.

She had strong religious beliefs about life and contraception and was totally stumped as to where to turn or what to do. Her estranged extended family was unsupportive and critical, and she believed they would chastise her for carelessly getting pregnant again. They would be no help in caring for the baby or helping with expenses. She was clear that she would not consider adoption; she wouldn't carry a baby to term, deliver, and turn the child out of the family. Her husband left the decision up to her. She wanted to know about the availability of a safe, legal abortion, and I shared with her what I knew. It was very early in her pregnancy and she grappled with her options, hating them all.

Ultimately, she chose to terminate the pregnancy, and her life seemingly went on as before. The next year they moved away, and when I saw her again, she had given birth to another baby—a beautiful boy with soft brown curls who was showing signs of mild developmental delay. As we sat over coffee, she wondered aloud if the child's disabilities were a punishment for her previous abortion. Did her son have to bear this burden because of her? Were she and her husband being punished? They loved and accepted him completely, but it caused her to speculate about the unborn child: would it too have had disabilities? Or would it have been "normal" – maybe even perfect?

I pondered my own role in the loss of her pregnancy. I felt like Saul in the Bible (Acts 7:54 - 8:2), an approving bystander at Stephen's stoning, holding the cloaks of those who cast the stones that killed him. What would I have done all those years ago if my period hadn't started and I *had* been pregnant?

The invitation to write this chapter re-opened memories, and I grappled with my own truth. It is easy to look in from the outside and smugly think you have all the answers. In fact, that is why many young women who are church goers quietly choose abortion rather than embracing a pregnancy that might bring them scorn and judgment or, at the very least, make them an easy target for church gossip.

Recently I watched a video depiction of Jesus and the woman caught in adultery, as told in John 8:2-11. As I watched, I was struck by Jesus' firm stance of love toward the woman and complete lack of judgment. The greedy crowd was itching to stone her, and the religious leaders were confident they would trap Jesus in a contradiction of their Law. Jesus took his time in responding, and ultimately all her accusers slunk away. Only she was left to face the Lord. And when she told him no one else condemned her, he assured her that he did not condemn her either. He then told her to go and to not sin anymore.

We are told in Romans 8:1 that there is no condemnation for those who are in Christ Jesus. His sacrifice on the cross has freed all who believe in Him from the guilt and stain of sin (life choices that hurt us and others, and the omission of things that God has called us to do in faithfulness and love). But true repentance also consists of a turning away from those things that are not pleasing to God. The woman was told, "I don't condemn you. Go in your freedom and do not sin anymore."

It sounds as though we have a choice: remain in our guilt and shame or choose life by believing in God's great love for us in sending His son to bear our guilt. When we look to Him in faith, we are washed clean. "*Therefore, if anyone is in Christ Jesus, the new creation has come: The old has gone, the new is here!*" (2 Corinthians 5:21)

Let every one of us choose life and live.

Editor's Note

by Sara Davison

A few years ago, I stood knee-deep in the Atlantic Ocean off the Canadian east coast as waves crashed around me and onto the shore. The sound was deafening, drowning out the cries of seagulls overhead and the laughing of children playing in the sand, well back from the reach of the pounding surf. The waves buffeted me so that occasionally I was nearly pushed off my feet. Yet I couldn't bring myself to come out of the water. I was mesmerized by the ocean, its wildness and power, the knowledge that, if I took a few more steps, I could be caught in its grasp and swept out to sea and lost forever. No human can withstand the force of the ocean. It silences and reduces to awe all who behold it.

But in spite of its intimidating power, there is one whose power is greater. When Job questions God after all the calamities that have fallen upon him and his family, God does not explain himself. Instead, he asks Job a series of questions, including this one: *"Who shut up the sea behind doors when it burst forth from the womb, when I made the clouds its garment and wrapped it in thick darkness, when I fixed limits for it and set its doors and bars in place, when I said, 'This far you may come and no farther; here is where your proud waves halt'?"* (Job 38:8-11)

I'm sure in every generation, in every society since the dawn of man, movements form that can become increasingly difficult to stand up to. In the face of them, silence is certainly the easiest recourse.

When I stood in those waves, I could have thrown back my head and hollered until my throat was raw, but few would have heard me. I would have simply looked foolish, standing there up to my knees in roiling water, waves sending me stumbling backwards, face red with exertion. Still, had I persevered, a person or two walking by on the shore might have caught something of what I said. And possibly they would have waded closer to hear more of the words, to attempt to understand the message I was trying to convey.

If they came close enough, we might even have been able to exchange thoughts and ideas. Possibly our conversation would have attracted the attention of a few more people who gathered around and joined in. With others now standing shoulder to shoulder with me, maybe my footing would have been more sure, and I would no longer have been driven back occasionally by the force of the waves. Eventually, our collective voices could very well have gained the power to rise above the roaring of the waves. None of us would be silent because together we had amassed a voice that could actually be heard.

And so it is with this book. One voice, one person, sharing his or her story might carry a little ways on the wind. But many voices joining together, refusing to be silenced, can swell into a resounding roar heard for miles. Or around the world.

For too long now I have been silent. My heart has broken at the thought of the thousands, the hundreds of thousands, the millions of tiny voices forever silenced by abortion. But the thought of speaking up can be overwhelming, even terrifying at times. At some point, however, a believer in the God who set the boundaries of the buffeting waves must make a choice, to remain silent or to stand up and say, along with the Creator of the universe—the one who formed each of those tiny babies with his own hands and in his likeness—"This far you may come and no farther."

I can think of no circumstances under which our loving and holy God, to whom each of those tiny, unborn children is precious, would condone their sudden, violent, intentional deaths. No matter how each was conceived, regardless of the ability of the mother to take care of or raise that child, it is unthinkable that it could *ever* be acceptable to the God who always, always stands on the side of the vulnerable, to callously and brutally end that innocent child's life.

I can also not think of a single circumstance under which that God would condone anyone directing judgment or hostility at the women carrying those children—women who are often desperate, usually young, sometimes the victims of violence themselves, almost always alone and without support or resources.

When the religious leaders brought the woman caught in adultery before Jesus, he did not defend her actions. As God, he was the one who had instituted laws regarding the sanctity of marriage, a holy estate in his eyes. Yet he showed grace and mercy toward this woman who must have been terrified, humiliated, desperate, and alone. He acknowledged that she had sinned and gently instructed her not to sin anymore, but he treated her with dignity, respect, and compassion while reminding her would-be accusers that none of us is without sin.

Grace and Truth. Mercy and Holiness. Only God can hold these in perfect tension. And yet believers are called to follow his example in this, as in all things.

The women and men who have shared their stories in this book have shown tremendous courage in doing so. Their stories are hard to read. The most heart-wrenching truth that emerges over and over from the pages is that, had they received support, had they been told by adherents of either the pro-choice or the pro-life sides that they truly *had* a choice, that other, viable options existed, that help and support were available, that whatever they chose, neither side would condemn them, they may very well have made a different decision. They might have chosen life and their little ones could have been given the opportunity to live out the futures God had planned for them, the chance to fulfill His purpose for them on earth.

Adherents to both sides of the issue are often at fault in not providing that unconditional support, those choices, that acceptance. So often women are lied to—they are told the child growing inside them is merely a clump of tissue, not a human being, they are told abortion is a simple solution to an inconvenient problem. They are not told that they are carrying a living person inside them and that going against every natural, God-given instinct to fight for and protect that tiny child by allowing it to be ripped in pieces from their bodies will greatly impact them physically, spiritually, emotionally, and psychologically for the rest of their lives.

If neither the pro-life nor the pro-choice side acts out of love, respect, and compassion for these women and offers them the support they need both before and after the birth of their child, or after they choose to end the pregnancy, if they fail to encourage them to consider other options such as adoption, or do not treat them with the love and dignity they deserve as those also created in the image of and loved by God, then both sides have failed them. And neither has the right to cast any stones.

The stories in this book, representing millions more all over the globe, call on every human being to set aside movements and ideology and agendas and hostility and begin to see these precious women and their innocent, unborn children not as pawns, but as persons worthy of dignity and respect.

Yes, we must take a stand. But we must do so in a way that makes it clear to every person contemplating or having had an abortion that they are loved, they have a voice, they are precious in the sight of God, and they can be forgiven and experience the freedom and joy that comes from laying the past at the feet of God and stepping into a future filled with hope.

Only then can we hope to change the endings of the countless stories that have yet to be written.

Resources*

Facing an unplanned pregnancy can be overwhelming, but please know that you are not alone. To locate free and confidential support, please research services in your area online, or visit the following:

- CHOICE42.com – www.choice42.com/resources
- Canadian Association of Pregnancy Support Services (CAPSS) – engaging the church in conversations with post-abortive women – www.capss.com
- Silent No More – www.silentnomoreawareness.org
- Save the One – www.savethe1.com
- Lifesite – www.lifesitenews.com/resources/abortion/get-help
- Birthrite.org – International 24-hour help line – 1-800-550-4900 www.birthright.org/learn
- Optionline – www.optionline.org
- Heartbeat International – www.heartbeatinternational.org

Please do not let your situation keep you from the available services provided by caring people. Reach out to a local pregnancy crisis centre or church and find one that offers you all the options and support without judgement.

*This list is intended as a guideline, a place to begin looking for the help and support you need. *Words To Inspire* is not officially affiliated with the organizations, homes, centres, or agencies listed in our database, nor is it responsible for any help, advice, or services offered by any of the above.

The WOW series
Coming Soon by Ruth Coghill:

Also Available
in the WOW series:

Woman of Worth!   *Woman of the Word!*   *Woman of Wisdom!*

For more information go to:
www.wordstoinspire.ca

To contact Ruth:
ruth@wordstoinspire.ca

Also by Sara Davison:

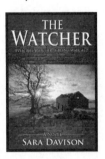

The first time Kathryn Ellison sees Nick Lawson, she knows there is something between them. He is too close, though, too involved with what happened to her the night that changed her life forever. As much as she wants to be with him, she wants even more to forget, to put the pain of the past behind her. When Nick shows up at her door twenty years later, Kathryn realizes it is finally time to move on with her life.

Over the next six days, she goes through the contents of the old shoebox in her closet, reliving and letting go of the memories contained in the old letters and photographs that have held her—and her daughter Lexi—captive for so long.

David Henley is a captive, too—of the dark secret he keeps from his wife and family. When Kathryn's daughter demands to know the truth about what happened That Night, the fragile peace he has worked so hard to achieve is threatened, and he is forced to confront the reality that he may lose everything in his life that is important to him.

As Kathryn and David struggle to deal with the past, Kevin Dylan, the man who has haunted Kathryn's dreams for twenty years, escapes from prison. He has always considered what happened That Night to be unfinished business, and now he is determined to come back and finish it.

Unaware of the approaching danger, Kathryn shuts herself away in her house and gradually works through the contents of the box. She is not as alone as she thinks she is, though. Someone, or something, is watching…

The Seven Trilogy:

The End Begins

One of them is a prisoner, and one of them is free.
The same one.

"The first book in Davison's Seven trilogy grips the reader from page one and holds on until the very end. Meryn O'Reilly is a believable character, and-though dreadful-the story is plausible. The events unfold in a forward-moving way that allows readers to sympathize with Meryn and Jesse and understand the dilemmas they face. Thought-provoking, relevant and suspenseful, *The End Begins* is a must-read." *-ROMANTIC TIMES*, 4 ½ Stars, Top Pick

The Darkness Deepens

Their secrets protect them ...
but secrets are hard to keep.

"The second book in the Seven trilogy is more exciting than the first... The suspense is well-paced and the timing is spot on, giving readers enough breaks to not be overwhelmed while never losing the tension." *-RT Book Reviews*, 4 Stars

"*The Darkness Deepens* is a riveting, well-written novel with an engaging storyline... Davison is a master at weaving the faith elements of he story into a beautiful tapestry that highlights rather than detracts from the underlying message of survival in a dangerous new world of unbelief. Readers will not be disappointed in the trilogy. It delivers!" Luana Ehrlich, Author of *Titus Ray Thrillers*

The Morning Star Rises

In the midst of all the fear and confusion, only one thing is clear ...
This isn't over yet.

"The final installment of Davison's Seven trilogy does not disappoint. The sense of foreboding is palpable .... Davison answers many mysteries presented throughout the series, all culminating in a shocking and satisfying end." -RT Book Reviews, 4 Stars

"Another thrilling read from Sara Davison. Thrust into the midst of intrigue, terror, and a heartrending love story, you will sit on the edge of your seat. Sara propels the reader into the battle between good and evil, where Christians must choose-Christ or their life. Don't miss this final episode in The Seven trilogy." -Bonnie Leon, Best-Selling Author of the Northern Lights series

The Night Guardians Series:

Vigilant

She must choose between the man who represents the law and the one who may have taken it into his own hands.

"In *Vigilant*, Sara Davison has created deep characters and a story that will grab your heart and keep you on the edge of your seat. Days after reading the story, the characters are still on my mind."-Patricia Bradley, Memphis Cold Case Series, Winner of Inspirational Readers' Choice Award

"*Vigilant* is a unique boundary-breaking suspense full of emotional depth. Davison's thought-provoking style will leave you breathless as you grapple with tough moral issues long after the story is over." -Rachel Dylan, Bestselling Author of the Atlanta Justice series

Coming soon: ***Guarded*** and ***Driven***